6: Peking, Moscow, and Beyond:
The Sino-Soviet-American Triangle

THE WASHINGTON PAPERS

6: Peking, Moscow, and Beyond: The Sino-Soviet-American Triangle

William E. Griffith

THE CENTER FOR STRATEGIC AND INTERNATIONAL STUDIES
Georgetown University, Washington, D.C.

1973

CONTENTS

"Roll up the map of Europe; we will not need it again in our lifetimes." Thus said Sir Edward Grey in August 1914. Now that President Nixon has been in Peking and Moscow and has mined Haiphong, must we roll up the map of the world and design a new one? Not a totally new one—but a changed one indeed.[1] This essay analyzes these recent Sino-Soviet-American developments and provides a brief, provisional survey of their regional implications.

PART ONE:

Sino-Soviet American Relations

The Sino-American Rapprochement

China's move toward the United States was implicit in the Sino-Soviet split.[2] Once the split occurred, and given China's weakness vis-à-vis rising Soviet hostility, the 1968 Soviet invasion of Czechoslovakia and the 1969 massive Soviet military deployment on its northern and western frontiers, its own overwhelming inferiority to Moscow in nuclear weapons, and Moscow's scarcely concealed threats to use them against China, all required that it improve its relations with Moscow's opponents, and above all with Washington.

This improvement was also furthered by Peking's realization that the American threat to its security was declining as a result of President Nixon's drastic wind-down of U.S. ground troop strength in Vietnam and, more generally, of the U.S. partial disengagement from Asia, as formulated in the "Nixon Doctrine." It was additionally aided by Peking's perception of a rising Japanese threat to its security and, moreover, by its offensive objectives: first, to prevent Japan from replacing the United States in Asia; second, to weaken the Japanese-American alliance; and third, to profit from U.S. disengagement in Asia. Specifically, Peking hoped to make progress toward the recovery of Taiwan, and at least to prevent the United States from accepting or furthering predominant Japanese influence on the island. Finally, the end of the Cultural Revolution, the purge of all his

opponents, and his recent return to a moderate domestic policy, also influenced Mao to move toward the United States.

Détente between Peking and Belgrade, which preceded and presaged the Sino-American rapprochement, began immediately after the August 1968 Soviet invasion of Czechoslovakia. Sino-American rapprochement was also foreshadowed by the Chinese resumption of diplomatic relations with Western European countries and Canada, and by Peking's willingness to improve relations with revisionist but anti-Soviet West European Communist parties.

The U.S. move toward China was the second major cause of the Sino-American détente.[3] In spite of the previous century of relatively good relations between the two powers, post-1949 Sino-American relations had been extremely hostile because of U.S. support of Chiang Kai-shek, Communist China's ties with the Soviet Union (the United States' main enemy) and, more generally, because of mutual, largely ideologically based suspicion. Chinese intervention in the Korean War, triggered by Peking's fear that the United States would not only conquer its ally, North Korea, but also attack China itself, greatly intensified Sino-American hostility. Moreover, the domestic political aftermath of the Korean War in the United States led to the incorrect, irrational conviction by much of the American right wing that "China had been lost" by procommunist American officials. All these developments made American presidents of both parties reluctant to advocate improvement in Sino-American relations based on mutual concessions until the late 1960s.

Two other factors made Washington delay détente with Peking. The first was the slowness of Washington policy makers to realize the depth and implications of the Sino-Soviet split, which began in the mid-1950s and reached the "point of no return" by 1959. Only in the early 1960s, however, was this fully realized in all Washington policy-making circles. Even then a tendency still continued, in the Kennedy and Johnson administrations, to give priority to bilateral U.S. détente with Moscow rather than to take advantage of the Sino-Soviet split by improving relations with Peking. United States support of India against China in 1962 also intensified Mao's anti-American

attitude. Finally, Johnson and his associates thought that China was behind the hostilities in Indochina and therefore viewed that war's main objective to be the containment of Chinese expansionism.

Nixon reversed U.S. policy toward China from confrontation to détente for two major reasons: the rise of Soviet military power and the American wind-down in Vietnam. Washington and Peking were both concerned over the former, and common concern over the same threat has always been the most effective impulse toward détente. American security, the Nixon administration felt, was increasingly threatened by the Soviet strategic and naval buildup, particularly when domestic support for U.S. military expenditures was declining. Moreover, Washington believed that Moscow had made dangerous advances in influence in Egypt and India for which it must compensate.

Nixon's winding down of the Vietnam War was the second major reason for improved relations with China. The President knew that because of the American public's disillusionment and war-weariness over a long and unsuccessful war he had no alternative but to do so, and specifically to end U.S. ground combat activity there. (He intended, however, through continued use of U.S. air and sea power, to so end the war that South Vietnam would not fall under Hanoi's control.) He hoped that rapprochement with Peking (and Moscow) might influence Hanoi toward peace without victory—as it did. He felt that rising Soviet power, declining U.S. military presence in Asia, and diminishing U.S. public support for overseas commitments could best be compensated for (and stability in Asia and the world best furthered) by a U.S. balance of power policy vis-à-vis Moscow and Peking, and in particular by improving U.S. relations with Peking to counterbalance Moscow's rising power.

Peking and Washington had been making preliminary gestures of rapprochement since late 1967. The 1970 invasion by the United States and South Vietnam of Cambodia and later of Laos only postponed their détente. It came in 1971.

The visit of President Nixon to Peking, his meeting with Chairman Mao there, and the massive U.S. television coverage of the entire visit improved the American image of China, and, one may assume, the Chinese view of the United States. Second, Washington and Peking agreed to disagree on Taiwan. In its most significant concession, Washington declared for the first time that it would not challenge the view of all Chinese that Taiwan is a part of China, i.e., it in effect abjured U.S. support for Taiwanese independence and potential Japanese hegemony over the island. The most significant Chinese concessions were only implicit: the Chinese did not mention the United States-Taiwan defense treaty, i.e., they implicitly agreed to tolerate its continuance. In addition, Peking welcomed Nixon, in spite of the continued, if sharply reduced, U.S. military presence in Vietnam, and the absence of a settlement there. Finally, both Peking and Washington declared that neither sought hegemony in East Asia and would oppose any attempt by another power (i.e., the Soviet Union) to attain it.

The most important results of the visit were two: it deepened Soviet uncertainty as to what the United States would do if Moscow were to attack China, and thereby more effectively deterred Moscow from doing so; and it made the Soviet Union intensify détente with Washington lest the United States further intensify its rapprochement with Peking to Moscow's disadvantage or, even worse from the Soviet Union's viewpoint, lest Washington aid and arm China against it.

The visit had several other significant results. The Chinese no longer needed to fear serious U.S. pressure against them and could thereby more effectively reactivate their foreign policy. They made themselves more respectable with states whose goodwill they wanted, although at the cost of damaging their revolutionary image with radicals throughout the world. They sullied that image further by their inaction in the face of U.S. mining and bombing of North Vietnam—but they could console themselves that Soviet inaction had sullied Moscow's image even more. They had to abandon their policy of total anti-American-ism. They did not succeed in allying with Washington against Moscow. As for the United States, it could more easily scale down its Asian commitments since it had less need to fear that Chinese expansionism would profit thereby. It strengthened the status quo in Asia to its own benefit. As subsequent Chinese inaction showed, Washington gained a freer hand in Vietnam from both Soviet and Chinese pressure. Nixon also acquired considerable credit abroad for détente with Peking, and benefited substantially both in domestic political prestige and in foreign policy flexibility. Indeed, he was thereafter no longer under any significant domestic pressures with respect to his China policy. The end of total Chinese anti-Americanism improved the American image in China. Finally, as a result of the Peking visit, the United States intensified its détente with Moscow and further deepened Sino-Soviet hostility to Washington's benefit. On the negative side, Washington allowed its relations with Japan (of which more below) to deteriorate gravely, and in my view unnecessarily, to Peking's (and Moscow's) profit.

The Soviet-American Conflict: Nature and Limitations

I begin with two, only apparently contradictory theses. First, as Michel Tatu has pointed out, post-1945 Soviet-U.S. hostility was always potentially less extreme that that between China and Russia. The United States and Russia neither border on each other nor have ever been opponents in war. Until 1917 they were basically friendly since they both feared other powers, first Great Britain and then Germany. After the brief and unsuccessful U.S. military intervention in Russia in 1919, capitalist America and communist Russia were ideologically but not militarily hostile. More importantly, neither was primarily preoccupied with the other and both were on the periphery not in the center, of world politics.[4]

Second, after 1945 the Soviet-U.S. cold war was in my view structural and inevitable. Western Europe and Japan were power vacuums. The Soviet Union was weak, desirous of maximum security, and by tradition and ideology expansionist. The United States, although strong, feared chaos and communism in Western Europe and Japan, and wanted a stable, free-trade world to insure its security and facilitate its economic expansion. Since all the other powers were so weak, the world was effectively bipolar, and multistate balance of power stability was therefore impossible. Moreover, the Soviet Union was for historic and ideological reasons so unattractive to Eastern Europe, Germany, and Japan, both as a domestic model and as a hegemonic power, that only Soviet military power could enforce its rule. Stalin, like other Russian rulers, regarded the existence of "friendly" (which for him could only be communist) governments in Eastern Europe as essential to Soviet security and to providing a secure jumping-off place for further expansion, should that become possible.

But Soviet acquisition of nuclear weapons, consolidation of its rule over Eastern Europe, the rapid American-aided and protected recovery of Western Europe and Japan, and the resultant realization in both Washington and Moscow of the necessity of limiting their conflict relationship, slowly but surely led to partial Soviet-American détente. All American administrations beginning with Eisenhower and all Soviet leaders after Stalin followed this policy. It resulted in the willingness of both Washington and Moscow to accept the status quo in Europe, contributed to the collapse of the Soviet alliance with China, and temporarily weakened the American alliance with Western Europe.

Détente also produced a feeling in Washington and Moscow in the 1960s that the two superpowers should settle major world problems between them. This attitude made each neglect its allies' interests. This mood continued on the part of the United States and, more understandably, on the part of the Soviet Union after the Sino-Soviet split had made it obsolete for American although not for Soviet policy. Nixon's recognition of this and his turn to a balance of power policy marked the real break in recent American foreign policy. Mao, who had always and naturally been opposed to it, also decided at the same time, for the reasons set forth above, to adopt a balance of power policy.

Nixon's visit to Peking was the first major new development in world affairs in 1972. The second was Vietnam: Hanoi's conventional invasion of the South, the retaliatory American mining and bombing of North Vietnam, the Soviet (and Chinese) inaction thereafter, and the Washington-Hanoi near-agreement on peace. Like the Nixon visit to Peking, Vietnam did not interfere with, and in my view even probably favored, the Nixon visit to Moscow, the subsequent (fourth) Kissinger visit to Peking, and the resultant intensification of Soviet-U.S. (and Chinese-U.S.)

détente. Hanoi probably, but vainly, hoped that its attacks and the U.S. response would sabotage the Moscow summit meeting and Soviet-American (and Sino-American) détente. But, as in the Caribbean in 1962, the Soviets in 1972 were very inferior in Southeast Asia in conventional air and naval power. Moreover, had the Soviets moved toward a confrontation with the United States over the American mining and bombing of North Vietnam, or even only postponed or cancelled the Nixon visit to Moscow, the Soviet-West German treaty, whose ratification was then still hanging in balance in the Bundestag, would have been postponed and very likely rejected; the Berlin agreement would therefore also not have been ratified; and thus Soviet détente policy in Europe would have been wrecked. Further, Moscow presumably calculated that any Soviet retaliatory move against Washington would have ruined the prospects for a SALT agreement and, worse, played into the hands of the Chinese by moving Washington closer to the Chinese. Finally, Moscow (and Peking) could hope that Hanoi would eventually take over Saigon and thus the Soviet (and Chinese) inaction in 1972 would be outshadowed by Hanoi's, and therefore Moscow's (and Peking's) defeat of the United States. In any case, Brezhnev overruled and demoted his hawkish opponent Shelest and the summit went forward.[5] (Similar considerations prompted the Chinese inaction as well.) Nixon's successful manipulation of the Soviets and the Chinese against each other thus enabled him to mine and bomb their North Vietnamese ally with impunity and simultaneously to intensify détente with both.[6] Moreover, as did the 1962 Cuban crisis, this undermined the credibility of Moscow and Peking with their allies and enemies and increased American credibility with its allies and enemies. Finally, it moved Hanoi toward peace.

The Soviet Union now regards the United States as the most powerful but the potentially less dangerous of its two major enemies, for it sees China, although weaker, as totally and inveterately hostile, at least as long as Mao and Chou remain in power. Bilateral Soviet-American relations have centered in three areas: strategic weapons, Europe, and the Middle East.

Three developments led to SALT.[7] The first was the threatening technological destabilization of the strategic arms race by MIRV and ABM. Both were technologically very sophisticated. They were not inspectable by purely national means (as missiles are by artificial satellites). Finally, they raised the spectre of first-strike capability: ABM by potentially protecting cities and missile sites against a second strike and MIRV by its greater number of warheads and its potentially greater accuracy. The qualitatively higher level of its technology made the United States likely to benefit more than the Soviet Union from this transfer of the arms race from quantity (missile launchers) to quality (MIRV).

But this was counterbalanced by the second development: the rise of the Soviet Union to thermonuclear parity with the United States. Although previous such Soviet rises in strategic power had always triggered a greater U.S. counterdeployment, this now only partially occurred. Although the United States did continue MIRV deployment, and, intentionally or not, may have regained—if only briefly—strategic superiority,[8] Washington seemed prepared to accept strategic parity with the Soviet Union, even though this might somewhat inhibit U.S. conventional freedom of action and make the Soviet Union tend toward a higher level of risk-taking.[9] It did so for three reasons: to maintain overwhelming superiority would be very costly; U.S. public opinion was far from enthusiastic about such a policy; and parity would permit lower levels of strategic deployments and therefore enable more funds to be transferred to domestic expenditures. The same reasons probably impelled the Soviet Union toward a partial SALT agreement based on parity.

The high point in Soviet-U.S. relations to date has been the May 1972 Nixon visit to Moscow and the agreements reached there.[10] They gave Moscow American recognition of Soviet equality—a long-standing Russian goal. Moscow also thereby got recognition of its strategic parity with the United States, made more certain that the United States would not ally with China against it, further consolidated détente in Europe (of which more below), made a Middle East confrontation less likely (albeit at the calculated risk of crisis with Cairo), and moved toward improving its technological position. The inspectability of ABM by national (i.e., satellite) means enabled a Soviet-American agreement to freeze ABM deployment and thereby freed Moscow from the threat of having its offensive deterrent degraded by a massive American ABM deployment. Conversely, the freeze on quantitative missile deployment freed the United States from the threat of continued Soviet SS-9 deployment and therefore of Soviet quantitative offensive superiority. (U.S. opponents of the SALT agreement maintain that the Soviets will eventually get MIRV and equivalent accuracy to the United States and then, given the greater SS-9 throw-weight, move toward superiority. Yet will new strategic technological discoveries ever end?) But Moscow, unsuccessful in allying with the United States against China, felt compelled to sit by idly while the United States mined and bombed North Vietnam, and, more generally, succeeded no more than Peking had in preventing or minimizing U.S. manipulation of Moscow and Peking against each other to American advantage.

By recognizing Soviet equality and intensifying détente, Washington hoped to confirm and institutionalize Soviet bureaucratic interests in détente. Through the Berlin agreement, it had defused the crisis area in which it was the most vulnerable. It no longer needed to be concerned about a Soviet confrontation over Vietnam and became less concerned about Soviet-U.S. confrontation in the Middle East. It preserved its ability to manipulate Moscow and Peking to its benefit. It maintained its technological qualitative lead in offensive weapons. Nixon profited domestically from his Moscow visit, as he had from his Peking trip. American debits were relatively minor. While Washington could hope that Moscow might lower its support to Hanoi, it could hardly expect that Moscow would try to force Hanoi to capitulate, and Moscow probably could not do so in any case. Détente in Europe, although it would initially ease congressional pressure for unilateral U.S. troop withdrawals (via Soviet agreement to MBFR negotiations), might well result in their gradual unilateral withdrawal in any case. Although a Soviet-U.S. Middle East confrontation was less likely, with what that involved in decline of Soviet influence in Egypt, long-range Soviet expansion in at least parts of the Arab world was likely to continue. The Soviet naval buildup would probably intensify after Moscow's humiliation off Haiphong. The Moscow agreement made Peking more likely to intensify its own détente with the United States.

Finally, as Michel Tatu noted, the Moscow summit officially codified the rules of coexistence. Whether it also marked, as Nixon and Kissinger hoped, the beginning of the institutionalization of bureaucratic pressures on both sides for détente remains to be seen.

The Soviet position in the Middle East (until July 1972) and South Asia had also improved. The Soviets were the most influential foreign power in Egypt, Syria, and Iraq, and also in India and Bangla Desh. Moscow had established air and naval bases and Soviet combat air deployment in Egypt. One might think, therefore, that Brezhnev had good reason to be content with his stewardship and to hope to go down in history, like Ivan the Terrible, Peter the Great, Alexander I, and Stalin, as a great builder of Russian imperial power, But, as the July 1972 Egyptian expulsion of the Soviet advisors showed, the Soviet position in the Arab world was far from firm. Worse, Brezhnev inherited from his predecessor, Khrushchev, the most pressing Soviet foreign policy problem, the crisis in Sino-Soviet relations.

The Sino-Soviet Split

Categorization of causes in international relations is inevitably stylized and artificial. Yet, as Kant pointed out, understanding events is otherwise impossible. I shall therefore divide the causes of the Sino-Soviet split into two general groups: geopolitical and organizational.[11]

Geopolitical factors. In retrospect, enduring Sino-Soviet comity, to say nothing of alliance, was never likely. The last fifteen years were one of those rare periods when a strong Russia and a strong China have confronted each other across common boundaries. Although postwar China cancelled the Western concessions and recovered control over all of its post-1911 territories, the vast pre-1911 Chinese territories annexed or controlled by the Russian Empire are still in Soviet hands. Any strong Chinese government was bound to see China's newly recovered glory as incomplete as long as one foreign barbarian state still occupied large areas of what was once formally Chinese territory. And although Mao knows that China is too weak to be able soon to recover them, like all Chinese rulers he thinks in the very long run indeed: he may well envisage their recovery when, as he likely expects, the Soviet empire eventually breaks up into its ethnic components.

Russia is a multinational state: nearly half of the Soviet population is not Great Russian. (Only six percent of China's is not ethnically Han.) The Soviets remember with apprehension the successful German subversion of many of their minorities in two world wars. On both sides of the boundaries between Soviet central Asia and Sinkiang and between Outer Mongolia and China, the inhabitants are not Great Russian or Han, but Kazakh, Uighur, and Mongol. There is a long history of Russian and Chinese intrigue among each other's minorities in this area. Sinkiang, overwhelmingly Uighur and Kazakh, was under effective Soviet control until 1949, and Outer Mongolia still is today. Since the late 1950s, when the Sino-Soviet dispute became serious, Moscow and Peking have both been trying to subvert the other's minorities in Soviet central Asia, Sinkiang, and even the Ukraine.[12] Thus the multinational character of both powers and the locations of their ethnic minorities further destabilize Russo-Chinese relations.

The Soviet Union and China are in very different stages of economic development. The Soviet Union is a highly developed country, notably in its industrial and military sectors, even if agriculture and housing are still backward. China is the largest underdeveloped country in the world. Furthermore, their revolutions are out of phase: the Soviet Union is in a Thermidorian period but China is still ruled by its original revolutionary elite. Finally, Mao is a Chinese nationalist, a revolutionary intellectual-in-arms, and an ascetic. He has usually insisted, at the cost of purge and turmoil, on a radical, antibureaucratic state. The post-Stalin leadership, conversely, has favored a technology-oriented, bureaucratic model of development.

The Soviet Union is a superpower whose decisive interests

center in Europe and whose principal traditional area of expansion has been southward toward the Middle East. China, a regional power and a weak atomic one, will long remain so underdeveloped that it cannot rival the Soviet Union or the United States in strategic or naval forces.

The Soviet and Chinese leaderships have also had conflicting foreign policies toward the United States, India, and Japan. For China, the Soviet Union preferred détente with the United States to risk-taking in China's interest (e.g., in the Quemoy and Matsu crises of the 1950s); supporting India in order to lower American influence there but also to contain Chinese influence in Asia; and more recently preferred rapprochement with Japan and the United States to détente with China (on China's terms). Conversely, for the Soviet Union, China has recently preferred détente with the United States, on a common anti-Soviet platform, to agreeing to Soviet proposals for a partial rapprochement. Finally, the nature of atomic weapons has worsened the Sino-Soviet alliance; for the Soviets, like the Americans, have been unwilling to give any of their allies significant atomic aid. Moscow did something even worse to the Chinese: it promised them atomic aid and then reneged on its promise.

Organizational factors. In Durkheim's terms, communism began as a sect but has now become a series of warring denominations. Its ideological fervor has largely given way to organizational and nationalistic considerations. Like Roman Catholicism, the domestic and international legitimacy of Communist ideology demands a centralized structure with one head. (But the Marxist doctrine of "proletarian internationalism" has turned out to be the emptiest myth; as the Sino-Soviet split has demonstrated, ours is an age of nationalism.) In addition, the international activity of Soviet and Chinese Communist parties (the "leading role of the CPSU" and the international attraction of Maoism to radicals) added to their state power. Conversely, loss of ideological legitimacy and organizational hegemony would worsen the positions of the Soviet and Chinese governments both at home and abroad.

Thus, both geopolitical and ideological considerations, as with Philip II of Spain, fuelled controversy. If one sees the Soviets as analogous to the seventeenth century Catholics and the Chinese to the Calvinists, one can better understand the dynamic of their factional struggle. Once Mao became convinced that Khrushchev was giving priority to Soviet national interests, especially détente with the United States, over Mao's version of "proletarian internationalism" (i.e., aid to China), he became convinced that Khrushchev was betraying not only China's national interests but communist doctrine as well. Moreover, Mao's turn in the late 1950s toward antibureaucratic extremism made him all the more ready to see in the Soviet leadership an "antimodel:" that bureaucratic degeneration and "restoration of capitalism" which he was determined to avoid in China.

Mao thus saw the Soviets as Luther and Calvin had seen Rome—as the (communist) antichrist. He therefore determined to replace Moscow with Peking as the center of communism. The resultant Sino-Soviet organizational struggle was, like the religious wars of the seventeenth century, a nationalistic as well as a sectarian one. Mao fought the Soviets not only on the state but also on the party level, by trying to split pro-Soviet Communist leaderships and parties and if this failed, to set up Maoist splinter groups which would claim to be the only legitimate Communist parties. As Sino-Soviet hostility accelerated, Moscow and Peking denounced each other as anti-Leninist and anti-Marxist. Each tried to overthrow the other's leadership, just as Philip II tried to overthrow Elizabeth of England. For mutual recognition of legitimacy is impossible in religious wars even if that religion, communism, be *ersatz* and secularized. For the orthodox, heretics are more dangerous than heathens.

Sino-Soviet tension reached its height in the 1969 border incidents. Thereafter, Moscow deployed a very large military force, more than a million men according to Chou En-lai, on the Sino-Soviet and Sino-Monoglian frontiers. Moscow intended minimally to intimidate the Chinese into a partial rapprochement. Some Soviet leaders probably advocated attacking China by conventional and perhaps even thermonuclear weapons if Peking proved recalcitrant; but so far they have not prevailed.

The Soviets decided on this massive troop deployment only after they had failed to get the Chinese to accept a partial détente in state relations and after Red Guard units had assaulted the Soviet Embassy and Soviet diplomatic personnel in Peking during the Cultural Revolution, and, worse, had instigated a series of border incidents against the Soviets culminating in the March 1969 incidents on Damansky/Chen Pao island on the Ussuri River. The Soviets retaliated in force there and in August in Sinkiang, and succeeded in compelling the Chinese to agree to begin what turned out to be fruitless border negotiations, but, more importantly, drove Peking toward Washington.

The Soviet military buildup on the Chinese frontier still continues and the Chinese have recently begun to redeploy troops to the north and west to counter it. Thus, after a century of threats primarily from the sea, China's historic security problem has returned: how to defend its northern and western boundaries against the foreign barbarians. Once it built the Great Wall; in 1972 it invited Nixon to walk along it. Both moves served to make these boundaries more secure.

The Sino-Soviet dispute also worsened organizationally. The course of the dispute has been cyclical, with periods of tension alternating with periods of apparently decreased tension. The latter, however, arose primarily from Soviet and Chinese desires to appeal to states and parties over which they were contending, all of whom did not favor a Sino-Soviet rupture. Until 1971 Chinese factional activity in the international communist and radical world was intense. When reformist tendencies and the Sino-Soviet struggle unsettled certain Communist parties in the developed world (notably in the Spanish, Japanese, and Australian ones), and when these parties condemned the 1968 Soviet invasion of Czechoslovakia, Moscow also began sponsoring factional minority groups, for example, against the Spanish and Australian party leaderships. In the case of the former, this coincided in time with, and was in part responsible for, moves by the Spanish, Italian, and Romanian parties toward rapprochement with Peking. These parties, although they preferred Moscow to Peking from the policy viewpoint, were not willing to endorse Moscow's extremist attitude toward Peking, because their own strivings toward autonomy and their struggle with their own left profited from Sino-Soviet détente rather than hostility.

Conversely, by 1971 Peking was ready, within the context of its reactivization of foreign policy and concentration on anti-Sovietism, to abandon its "exclusivist" attitude—its demand for total loyalty from its supporters and its rejection of "communist neutralism." Consequently, in 1971-72, with the support of the Romanian and Italian parties, the strongly rightist, revisionist Spanish Communist Party (PCE) sent a top-level delegation to Peking and the two parties agreed to disagree.[13] By this move on the party level, as by their rapprochement with Yugoslavia on the state level, the Chinese showed clearly how pragmatic their foreign policy in the communist world had become: they would ally with anyone, communist, revisionist, or capitalist, who was anti-Soviet. For Moscow, on the other hand, these Chinese moves made Sino-Soviet reconciliation all the less likely, for the Soviets were thereby confronted with the prospect of their enemies on the right and on the left uniting against them, i.e., with the communist equivalent of the Sino-American rapprochement. Soviet polemics toward China became even more violent and relations worsened further.[14] While the Soviets continued to want partial rapprochement with China, if only to make their military engagement on China's borders less burdensome and to deter Peking from moving too far toward Washington. Thus, by mid-1972, prospects for Sino-Soviet departure, in anticipation that a partial rapprochement would then occur, Mao remained adamant: he preferred détente with Washington. Thus, by mid-1972 prospects for Sino-Soviet détente, as long as Mao ruled in Peking, seemed slim indeed. What would happen after Mao, however, remained almost totally obscure. Even so, the Sino-Soviet geopolitical and organizational issues make a Sino-Soviet reconciliation unlikely, in my view, in the near future.

Conclusion

The now fashionable cliché, that international politics have become triangular, is, like all other *terribles simplifications,* only part of the story. First, there is not one triangle but two: the political-military triangle, composed of the United States, the Soviet Union, and China; and the economic triangle, composed of the United States, Western Europe, and Japan.

Second, these two triangles are asymmetrical and unstable. The first triangle is asymmetrical because China is so much weaker than the United States or the Soviet Union. It is unstable because Soviet military power continues to rise while U.S. military power, and the perceived will to use it (at least until the 1972 U.S. mining and bombing of North Vietnam), has continued in relative decline. China's smaller military power, especially in the strategic field, continues to rise, but slowly. The second triangle is asymmetrical because the U.S. economy is still much larger than that of either Western Europe or Japan. It is unstable because the U.S. economic position continues to decline compared to Western Europe and to Japan.

Third, both triangles are also complex and interrelated, because the political-military one is composed of limited adversaries and the economic one of limited allies. Only the United States is a member of both, but its position in one is in part determined by its position in the other, and its principal allies, Western Europe and Japan, are not only important ingredients of its political-military strength but also its major and increasingly successful economic competitors. Even so (and although atomic weapons, the balance of power, and economic competition have limited adversary and alliance relationships) the latter still remain primary for Washington and Moscow.

Fourth, because of Soviet and Chinese economic and technological weakness and Western European and Japanese military weakness, only the United States is a full member of, and therefore can maneuver in, both triangles. Only for Japan is there a realistic potentiality in the near future of being in both triangles. Neither the Soviet Union nor China seems likely to develop either the outward-thrusting economy or the technological sophistication to become a full member of the economic triangle, while Western Europe seems unlikely, because of French intransigence and West German reluctance, to become a major thermonuclear power and therefore a full member of the political-military triangle.

Fifth, most of the Third World remains sufficiently unstable and weak to tempt Moscow and Peking and also, although less so, Washington, to compete in it for power and influence. This is particularly true for Moscow and Washington in the Middle East, where China is little present; great power rivalry is therefore bipolar, and neither superpower can control its allies.

Finally, thermonuclear weapons limit and push forward superpower competition and limit alliances. They push forward competition because recent technological developments in thermonuclear weapons, notably MIRV, destabilize the arms balance. Thermonuclear weapons limit superpower competition because they cause mutual fear of atomic destruction, e.g., in the 1962 Cuban missile crisis, which led to partial Soviet-U.S. détente. But this détente also limited U.S. alliances, because its allies feared that it preferred partial détente with its enemies to full support of its alliances and because the United States was so reluctant to give its allies atomic aid. The same developments helped not to limit but to wreck the Sino-Soviet alliance. Finally, Sino-U.S. and Soviet-U.S. détente, coupled with Sino-Soviet hostility, prevents collusion of Moscow and Peking against Washington and favors Washington's manipulation of Moscow and Peking against each other. (One indeed wonders how long Peking will prefer this to a partial Sino-Soviet détente whereby it could maneuver between Moscow and Washington.)

Because, therefore, it is more complex, more asymmetrical, and more unstable, the present international balance of power is not, and cannot be, like its nineteenth century predecessor. The implications of these new and complex great power relationships for key regions of the world will be analyzed in the rest of this paper.

PART TWO:

The Regional Implications of Sino-Soviet-American Relations

Europe

The rising importance of civilian and military technology for economic, military and political power, and the instability and slowness of development of the Third World have made Western Europe and Japan increasingly more important in international politics, and the Third World less so. Other factors have also furthered this trend. Economically, both Western Europe and Japan are near equals of the United States and superior to the Soviet Union and China. Historically, post-1945 Soviet-American relations have centered in Europe—one of the two great prizes of World War II—and unlike Japan, the other prize, Europe has been divided between Soviet and American spheres of influence. A change in the alliance structure of these two areas would decisively transform East-West relations.[15]

Western Europe and the United States. Since the 1962 Cuban missile crisis, American and Soviet policies in Europe have moved toward détente and recognition of the status quo. Western Europe has become economically much more powerful. DeGaulle's departure, Pompidou's concern with Bonn's rising power, and Heath's determination all brought about the United Kingdom's entry into the EEC and the resumption of progress toward Western European monetary, financial, and perhaps even eventually partial political union. But Western Europe remains militarily weak because of a lack of West European unity and public will to increase military expenditures and because of two major obstacles to the creation of a European nuclear force—the only instrument that could make West Europe militarily, and therefore politically, a superpower. These obstacles are, first, the French reluctance to merge their national deterrent into a West European one, and, second and more important, the West German reluctance, especially of the SPD, to imperil Bonn's détente with Moscow in order to participate, even if only financially, in a West European deterrent. Neither obstacle seems likely to be overcome soon. Western Europe will therefore remain, in the near future, militarily weak and dependent for its security upon the U.S. nuclear guarantee and U.S. troop presence in Germany.[16] On the other hand, trade competition between the United States and the EEC, although not so serious as that between the United States and Japan, is increasing, and the American balance of payments and balance of trade deficits reinforce U.S.-EEC tensions. Moreover, Nixon's lack of consultation with Western Europe before his August 15, 1971, economic measures and Secretary Connally's Texan toughness in negotiations with them worsened U.S. relations with Western Europe as well as with Japan.[17] The forthcoming U.S.-EEC trade negotiations and the recurrent international monetary crises will have to be handled more diplomatically lest they still further worsen U.S. relations with Western Europe.

Eastern Europe and the Soviet Union.

Minimum Soviet security interests in Europe are to maintain Soviet hegemony, if necessary by military force, over Poland, Czechoslovakia, Hungary, and East Germany.[18] The wave of liberalization in Czechoslovakia in 1968, Moscow finally decided, required Soviet military intervention lest it spread to Poland, East Germany, and the Soviet Union itself. Although the Soviets skillfully handled the Polish seacoast riots of December 1970 by allowing Gierek to replace Gomulka and by giving him major credits, the shock to Moscow of so suddenly and unexpectedly being confronted by a spontaneous workers' rebellion must have been great. Moscow is thus under no illusions, and probably never was, that its hegemony over the northern tier of Eastern Europe will soon, if ever, be seen as legitimate by East Europeans. But its ruling elite's position, its imperial power, and particularly, given its multinational character, its domestic unity and stability are seen by the Soviet ruling elite to require Soviet maintenance. Moreover, Romania is still unreliable in Moscow's view, although Soviet-Romanian relations have somewhat improved.[19] Yugoslavia, although recently on better terms with Moscow, is still non-aligned, revisionist, and on good terms with Peking (but its post-Tito ethnic tensions seem promising for Soviet intrigue).[20] Albania is anti-Soviet and pro-Chinese, albeit troubled by Peking's rapprochement with Washington.[21] Hungarian economic reforms and East German intransigence also offer problems to Moscow.[22] Thus, the minimal Soviet position in Eastern Europe, although consolidated by military force, is still potentially unstable enough so that Moscow wants Western and particularly West German and American recognition of it. This recognition is probably now Moscow's chief minimal and defensive aim in Europe.

Moscow's second minimal defensive aim is to keep its western flank quiet while it confronts China to the east. Historically, Russia has always tried to avoid simultaneous war or tension on both its flanks. It has recently deployed a massive army on the Chinese frontier. As it always has, Russia fears encirclement; that all its enemies (China, America, Western Europe, and Japan) will combine against it. It fears most of all that the United States, or Western Europe, or Japan, or two or all three of them, will aid China technologically and therefore, in fact if not in design, arm it against the Soviet Union. It probably also fears not only the Sino-American rapprochement and American aid to a China hostile to Moscow, but also a Sino-German alliance on a revanchist, anti-Soviet platform. (Although this is not presently a danger for Moscow, some right wing German politicians give the Soviets ground for some rational and more irrational concern.) Moscow therefore realizes that in order to be certain to avoid a Sino-American alliance against the Soviet Union, it must avoid major East-West tension in Europe.

Moscow also has a third defensive aim in its intensification of détente in Europe: to decrease and if possible to reverse its rapidly growing technological gap with the West, especially in such frontier areas as computers and microelectronics. The gap arises in large part from Soviet secrecy and compartmentalization, both of which slow down spin-off from military to civilian industry, and from backwardness and overcentralization in industrial management and production. Since Moscow is politically unwilling to change these counterproductive policies, it must try to get large amounts of technology and credits from the West with which to pay them. The only western country that has technology, credits, and a strong political motive to give them is West Germany. Thus, Moscow expects its détente with Bonn to narrow its technological gap.

That the Soviet Union has these three minimal defensive motives in its *Westpolitik* is generally agreed among western experts. More debatable is whether Moscow is now also pursuing maximal, offensive aims in Europe. I shall consider this possibility under three headings: lowering or ending the U.S. presence in Europe, slowing down or reversing West European unification, and profiting from social tensions there.

As to the first, the Soviets would be happy with less American presence in Western Europe, and indeed would be glad to see it disappear entirely, but on one condition: that it not be replaced by a heavily armed German one. Soviet disinterest in MBFR shows that Moscow anticipates that it need only wait for U.S. presence to be reduced unilaterally. Moreover, the Soviets can reasonably hope to profit in Western Europe from their attainment of nuclear parity with the United States, from U.S. domestic crises, from U.S. absorption in Vietnam, and, more generally, from the fact that for many West Europeans the United States is no longer a model to be emulated but an example to be feared.

The Soviets have always opposed West European unification, including the United Kingdom's entry into the EEC, and have done what they could to slow it down. They would undoubtedly like to reverse the entry, but now seem prepared to accept it as a *fait accompli* and to deal with the Community, even though its forthcoming common foreign trade policy will make Soviet bilateral trade with West European countries more difficult.[23]

China, in contrast, now welcomes West European unity as a counterbalance against the two superpowers.[24]

Western European societies seem to be in a phase of crisis of authority which, although less marked than that in the United States, may still offer some opportunities for the Soviets, even in the context of what, considering Moscow's problems with its own dissidents, Leo Labedz is right to call "competitive decadence." In my view the Soviets will continue to give priority to their minimal defensive aims in Europe, and it is unlikely in the near future that the United States will withdraw to the point where Moscow will be tempted to concentrate on its maximal, offensive ones.

Sino-Soviet hostility in Europe is less obvious and less important than in Asia. Ever since the invasion of Czechoslovakia and the reactivization of their foreign policy, the Chinese have intensified their ties with what they hope will be—and what, indeed, largely already is—an anti-Soviet bloc in the Balkans; Romania, Yugoslavia, and Albania. Peking supported and urged on the Romanians against the Soviets. Swallowing its ideological hostility to Yugoslavia, it executed a rapprochement with Belgrade on purely and simply a common fear of Moscow. Moreover, there is some evidence—which the Soviets almost surely overrate—that the Chinese have been trying to subvert, via émigrés, the Ukrainians and Balts in the Soviet Union, as they clearly have the Soviet central Asians. In any case, the Chinese are sufficiently active and hostile in Europe so that Moscow is further influenced toward a détente with Washington and Bonn, and also with Yugoslavia and Romania.

The case of Yugoslavia is particularly significant within this context. After the Soviet-Yugoslav and Soviet-Romanian crises subsequent to the 1968 Soviet invasion of Czechoslovakia, China and Yugoslavia, Albania and Yugoslavia, and Romania and Yugoslavia all moved toward détente with each other, and Romania and Yugoslavia toward improvement of relations with Western Europe as well as the United States. But as post-1968 Yugoslav fear of Russia declined, intra-ethnic Yugoslav tensions revived and, by 1971, Croat separatism had become so serious that Marshal Tito felt compelled to suppress it. (He reacted, in my view, too sharply and too late, even for his own purposes.) At the same time Soviet-American and Sino-American détente began to intensify. Moreover, initially after 1968 the Soviets had likely been covertly involved with the separatist émigré Ustase and some pro-Soviet elements of the Serbian UDBA, making Soviet-Yugoslav tension in 1970 very serious indeed. More recently, Belgrade smashed an émigré Ustase terrorist band in Bosnia, and by late 1971 Moscow and Belgrade began to move again to rapprochement. The Soviets wanted to counter Chinese, American, and West German presence in Belgrade and to encourage Tito toward more repressive domestic measures. Tito, conversely, felt that Sino-American and Soviet-American détente but continuing Soviet-Yugoslav tensions would leave him too little freedom of movement vis-à-vis Moscow and therefore too dependent on the West. This, plus his concern over Croat separatism and his desire to deter the Soviets from interfering in tensions among Yugoslav nationalities, made him reciprocate the Soviet offer. Thus Tito regained domestic control and international flexibility. However, whether Yugoslavia can remain united and active in foreign policy after the eighty-year old Marshal leaves the scene is in my view even more doubtful than before Tito's harsh suppression of Croat nationalist dissidents. On the contrary, post-Tito Yugoslavia remains the most dangerous potential crisis point in Europe, one in which the Sino-Soviet-American relationship will probably continue to play a major role.

The main American interests in Western Europe are three: to prevent it from again becoming the source of international conflict; to deny it to Soviet hegemony; and to maintain U.S. trade and investment access to its markets. The United States is militarily so strong and Western Europe so weak that continued American military presence in Western Europe remains the only alternative to Soviet military, and therefore, gradual political predominance on the Continent. Yet Western Europe is increasingly seen by the United States as a dangerous economic competitor. Even, therefore, if the "post-Vietnam syndrome" in the United States does not result in major unilateral U.S. troop reductions in Western Europe, some more burden sharing in this respect and improvement of economic relations seem required in order to preserve the present state of U.S.-West European relations and U.S. military presence there. In any case, West European concern over declining U.S. and rising Soviet presence (its fear of "Finlandization") plus U.S.-EEC economic tensions and the negative effect of détente on the NATO defense posture will remain continuing problems for U.S.-West European relations.

In my view, the Soviet Union decided in 1970 to undertake a strategic détente in Europe. This led to the Soviet-West German and Polish-West German treaties and will now lead to a European Security Conference. A similar policy was adopted by the Brandt government in Bonn and, although initially less decisively, by the Nixon Administration in Washington. It was based upon mutual acceptance of the status quo, including the existing alliance systems, boundaries, states (including East Germany), and West Berlin. (The Soviet-West German and Polish-West German treaties were, on balance, advantageous to Moscow; the Berlin Agreement to the West.) Minimally, both wanted to intensify détente and thereby stabilize the status quo. But both Moscow and Bonn, and even Washington, accepted the status quo and intensified détente in order, maximally, to change it—what Egon Bahr has termed "change through rapprochement" *(Wandel durch Annäherung)*. In particular, Moscow wanted to stabilize East Germany. (East Berlin also wanted to isolate itself from the Federal Republic). At the same time Bonn wanted to increase contacts with East Germany and thereby potentially, although in a controlled manner, destabilize it, but to stabilize the position of West Berlin. Whether Bonn (and Washington) can, as they wish, control the inevitably destabilizing effects of détente in Central Europe, and specifically in East Germany, remains unclear. That Moscow and East Berlin can, and will, seems likely—if necessary by the Red Army.

The ratification of the treaties with Moscow and Warsaw by the Bundestag, even though by small majorities that left the Brandt government without a sure base of parliamentary power, marked the first stage in the Soviet and West German strategic détente. The Berlin agreements and the Bonn-East Berlin agreement reinforced this trend. The forthcoming European Security Conference will probably contribute further to the three minimal Soviet defensive aims outlined above, and, perhaps, to their maximal aims as well. Alternatively, depending on its outcome, it may well destabilize Eastern Europe. This will particularly be the case with respect to the two Germanies. For détente between them will intensify their political struggle—just as it will, more generally, between West and East. The result of this European race of competitive political decadence will be primarily decided by the relative degree of destabilization of East Germany (through rising contacts with West Germany) and on both the degree of destabilization of West Germany (through CDU-SPD hostility about *Ostpolitik*) and, perhaps more important, on radical currents within and to the left of the SPD and within the West German universities. (The danger of this in West Germany, although not yet great, certainly exists; the more so because a large part of radical West German students, uniquely in the world, are in fact disciplined Marxist-Leninists—anti-western, pro-DDR, and pro-Soviet—and exhibit many of the behavior patterns of the SA students of the early 1930s.)

The Soviets also agreed in Moscow to separate multilateral negotiations on mutual balanced force reductions (MBFR) in Europe, thus enabling Washington to stave off further senatorial pressure for unilateral U.S. troop cuts in West Germany and perhaps actually to achieve some mutual force reductions.

Moscow is also tightening up foreign policy coordination with its allies. It is annoyed by Chinese activity in the Balkans and elsewhere in Eastern Europe but is hardly endangered by it. It hopes that the United States will continue to turn inward and cut its commitments in Europe. But above all, it wants to keep Europe quiet while it pursues its expansionist aims in the Middle East and South Asia, and continues its confrontation with China.

The Middle East

The Middle East has been a major area of Soviet-American, but not of Sino-Soviet, confrontation.[25] Recent Sino-Soviet-American developments have greatly contributed to changes there, and especially to Sadat's July 1972 expulsion of many Soviet advisors from Egypt. Indeed, they should in part be seen as the second and most important regional result of recent Sino-Soviet-American developments. (The Korean détente, of which more below, was the first.) The relative absence of China in the Middle East may not continue indefinitely. Peking is trying to build up a Middle Eastern presence, and the future may offer the Chinese more opportunities there. The Sino-Soviet-American triangle thus has important implications for the Middle East, and the Middle Eastern states actively force the great powers to take specific attitudes. Egypt, Syria, Iraq, and South Yemen are not satellites of the Soviet Union. Israel is clearly not under American control. Middle Eastern politics has thus been a process of interaction between the local states and great powers, and at no time more so than in 1972.

In mid-1972, there were two new major dynamic trends dominating Middle Eastern politics: the improvement in the position of Israel and the sharp worsening of Soviet-Egyptian relations. In mid-1971 it still seemed to me that the rising Soviet military presence in Egypt, the American reluctance to provide Israel with more Phantoms, and the likely Egyptian resumption of raids across the Canal made Israel's security situation potentially more dangerous than at any time since the 1967 Six Day War. Although in my view some long-range danger to Israel remains and it has increasing domestic, economic, and social problems, its security position has significantly improved. This became even more the case after the other major new Middle Eastern development, the July 1972 Soviet-Egyptian crisis.

Israel's position also improved because of President Nixon's concern over rising Soviet power in the area, plus his wish to gain the Jewish vote and Jewish campaign contributions for the Republican Party in the 1972 Presidential elections and thereafter. Washington precently agreed to sell the Israelis 36 Phantoms. Effective U.S. pressure for Israel to withdraw from its conquered territories has ceased as of mid-1972. (Israel agreed to indirect negotiations with Egypt, but only with no commitment to evacuate the occupied territories and only at a time, after the recent Egyptian student demonstrations, when Sadat can hardly agree to them.)

Other recent Middle Eastern developments also favored Israel. By a sophisticated combination of military and political ruthlessness with rapid economic development, Israel "pacified" the West Bank and the Gaza strip. Hussein defeated the fedayeen, who are in major and probably prolonged disorder, despondent of Arab or Soviet help (and therefore the more likely to continue sporadic terrorism). His recent proposal for a federation of Jordan with the West Bank, although rejected by Jerusalem, was in fact a step toward a compromise peace with Israel. Soviet-Egyptian relations, as we shall see below, worsened sharply. The Shah, with whom Israel has good relations, established *de facto* hegemony in the Persian Gulf. Partly for that reason, Soviet and radical Arab expansion there has not as yet occurred. But the Gulf Sheikdoms remain unstable, and should one of them be radicalized, Moscow would surely be tempted to aid it. Their long-term prospects are hardly promising for the Sheikhs or for the West.[26]

The Israelis and Arabs both realize that Soviet inaction in the face of Nixon's mining and bombing of North Vietnam plus the U.S. "smart bombs" and improved electronic countermeasures (see below) further improve Israel's military situation and worsen Egypt's, deter the Soviets, and reinforce American will to support Israel. As a result of all the above developments plus the Lod and Munich massacres and what most Israelis perceived as Egyptian endorsement of them, the Israeli "doves" are silent, while the kibbutzim elite is rapidly becoming modernized (*inter alia* via kibbutzim industrial operations), self-confident, and more powerful. Part Prussian, part Spartan, part socialist, essentially a European state set down in the Middle East, Israel understandably now looks with confidence to the future. Finally, Moscow began to make covert feelers to Jerusalem for reestablishment of Soviet-Israeli diplomatic relations. And for the first time in Soviet history the Soviet Union began to allow a substantial number of Soviet Jews—in the thousands—to emigrate to Israel.

Conversely, the Arab position weakened. After Nasser's death much of the Arab world moved toward the right. This was caused by Nasser's death, by a revival of the traditionalist, Islamic, and xenophobic currents in Arab history, by continued Arab frustration over the failure of the Arab Left and their patrons, the Soviets, to push the Israelis out of any of the conquered territories, and most recently, by the Soviet back-down in Vietnam and by the complex issue of the July 1972 Soviet-Egyptian crisis which will be discussed further below. The Arab world did not, however, become more conservative. On the contrary, its long-range trend to radicalization will probably continue. By 1972 Arab radicalism had become, unlike Nasserism, primarily xenophobic and rightist, combining Islam with some, but less, social radicalism, and with anticommunism as well as antiwesternism. Qhadhafi of Libya was the initial example. Numeiry of the Sudan, after he crushed the recent communist connected coup, moved toward Washington and Peking.[27] Even Syria became less extreme. Most remarkably, in July 1972 Sadat himself, illustrating the same trend, expelled the Soviet advisors from Egypt.

Sadat moved to the right even though this worsened his relations with the Soviet Union.[28] He realized that renewed raids on Israel were prohibitively expensive and opposed by the Soviets, who gave priority to their own détente with Washington. Sadat, given his own more traditionalist orientation, saw no alternative but rapprochement with the disaffected Egyptian intelligentsia, whose mood remained cynical, bitter, and weary of war. He hoped, as it turned out vainly, also so to improve relations with the United States that Washington would pressure Israel out of at least some of the conquered Egyptian territories. But, as the July 1972 events clearly demonstrated, he had also to guard against a military coup by frustrated young officers, smarting like the demonstrating students under continuing Israeli humiliation, Soviet refusal to support Egyptian military action against Israel, and Sadat's own understandable refusal to start raids against the overwhelmingly militarily superior Israelis. Because he was impotent against continued Israeli occupation of Sinai and because he failed to get Washington to get the Israelis out of any conquered territories, he had to demand more Soviet military aid and allow Soviet military bases in Egypt, only to realize that the Soviets would not support him militarily against Israel. Instead, their presence in Egypt pushed Washington toward

Jerusalem and away from him. He therefore, by 1971 at the latest, began a gradual, cautious, partial disengagement from Moscow. He purged the pro-Soviet Ali Sabry and his associates. Like Nasser, he kept the Egyptian Communists impotent.[29] When pro-Communist officers in Khartoum overthrew Numeiry and Qhadhafi, on whom he depended for massive financial subsidies, Sadat aided Numeiry's countercoup in Khartoum, even though it worsened his relations with Moscow.

Sadat's July 1, 1972, expulsion of Soviet military advisors from Egypt is still too recent, and my information about its background is still too scanty, to allow more than a very preliminary analysis. He "requested" (i.e., compelled) the rapid withdrawal of some ten to fifteen thousand Soviet military advisors who were training the Egyptian army and supervising the SAM sites west of the Suez Canal, plus Soviet combat air personnel. The status of Soviet naval bases in Egypt remains unclear. Soviet economic aid personnel were at least initially not expelled. This enforced withdrawal, Sadat made clear, was a result of Moscow's refusal to give Egypt the offensive weapons against Israel that Sadat wanted: long-range bombers and intermediate-range missiles and, very likely, to allow what weapons Moscow had given him to be wholly under Egyptian control. In short, Moscow refused to guarantee Cairo the use of its military aid and the aid of the Red Air Force units in Egypt so that Egypt could with confidence resume hostilities against Israel.

Sadat probably chose this move because he saw it as the lesser of two evils—the other being to resume raids across the Canal in the sure expectation of devastating Israeli retaliation. He felt that he had to choose one or the other, one may assume, because if he did nothing he faced the prospect of a military coup. Given the frustration of the Egyptian military, many of whose younger officers wanted to fight Israel; the frustration (of a different kind) of the more moderate intelligentsia, many of whom wanted peace;[30] the educated Egyptians' hatred of the "ugly Russians," whose contempt for the Egyptians, however justified, was glaringly obvious; the Russian back-down before Nixon off Haiphong; the potential strengthening of Israel by the "smart bombs" and ECM; the Soviet welcome to Nixon in Moscow, where (or so Sadat probably thought) the Russians agreed with the Americans to keep the peace in the Middle East, which for Cairo meant to maintain the Israeli occupation of Egyptian territory; plus the anti-Soviet pressure on Sadat by Qhadhafi and Numeiry—given all this is it any wonder that Sadat decided to retaliate against Moscow? Not, it seemed initially, that he intended to break with Moscow, from whom he still needs military and economic aid. But he probably felt that he could still get this aid and also renew negotiations with the United States, the only power that can force Israel out of its conquered Egyptian territory and give Egypt massive economic aid, and also with West Europe, notably France, which disagreed with total U.S. support of Israel and which might potentially aid the Egyptians. After all, if the French sold Mirages to Libya, why should they not sell them to Egypt?[31]

Beginning with the Ptolemies, Egypt has always been dependent on a foreign power. After its disillusionment with Moscow, which frustrated its main national goal—the recovery of its conquered territories and the overcoming of its humiliation at the hand of the hated, despised Israelis—the best that Cairo can hope for, many educated Egyptians probably now feel, is to be dependent on and balanced between more than one foreign power. So Sadat probably calculated. Yet above all he had to survive; to guard against a military coup by taking the popular course of moving against the hated Russians, who would not attack him, rather than against the much more hated Israelis, who certainly would.

Yet in the long run it did not solve but only postponed his problems. First, as to Washington: Nixon, with his initial cultivation of Sadat and subsequent support of Israel, his facing down and then negotiating with Moscow, was certainly not willing to pressure Israel for evacuation before the presidential elections. Nor was he very likely to do so effectively thereafter because he needed to be far less concerned about a Soviet-American confrontation in the Middle East (or elsewhere). Nor would the Israelis make concessions to Egypt. After Haiphong,

Moscow, and the departure of the Russian advisers, Sadat was militarily weaker than before. Moreover, Jerusalem had learned that the best way to meet pressure from Washington was to stand firm.

Thus, by expelling the Soviet advisors, Sadat had postponed the danger of a coup, regained much popularity, improved his relations with Tripoli, Khartoum, Washington, Peking, and Paris, and retained a good bargaining position with Moscow. However, he made little if any progress toward solving his key problem of regaining at least some of the conquered Egyptian territory. But he could not do that anyway with or without Moscow, and at least he had gained time.

Until July 1972 the Soviet position in the Middle East, historically an area of major defensive and offensive interest to Russia, had greatly improved since the 1967 Six Day War.[32] Arab frustration and radicalization and resultant anti-westernism,[33] even after Sadat's turning against them, was likely to continue to Soviet profit. Yet recently the Soviets ran into major difficulties in the Arab Middle East: the Arab trend toward the right; the countercoup in the Sudan; the Arab Union of Egypt, Libya, and Syria, a rightist and partially anti-Soviet grouping; Qhadhafi's frenetic anticommunism and the billions of dollars he has to further it; Sadat's purge of Ali Sabry and other pro-Soviet Egyptian leaders, his open support of the Khartoum countercoup and the resultant decimation of the strong Sudanese Communist Party, and his approaches to the United States; greater moderation in Syria; the negative repercussions of the Soviet back-down in Vietnam and their agreements with Nixon in Moscow; and, last and worst of all, the humiliating expulsion by Sadat of the Soviet advisors. The Soviets had for some months before been trying to compensate for all these developments, and especially for their worsening relations with Egypt, by shifting their attention from Egypt toward increasing Soviet and Communist influence in the Baath governments in Syria and Iraq. But the Communists there remained relatively weak and in Syria the ruling Baath faction increasingly showed moderation. Only in Iraq, still unstable and isolated, did Moscow recently increase its influence.[34]

Several other developments added to Soviet difficulties in the Middle East. The extent to which they deemed it useful to support the Arabs remains doubly limited: they dared not support them too much against Israel, lest this lead to a military confrontation with the United States, which they wished to avoid more than ever. Yet if they supported them too little, as with Sadat, the Arabs moved to the right and, worse, toward the United States and China. The Soviets continued to see long-term opportunities in the unstable Persian Gulf sheikdoms, which include the world's richest oil deposits, upon which Western Europe and Japan depend heavily, and from which the United States draws great financial advantages. But the Shah made it clear that the Gulf is his area of hegemony and Moscow has so improved its position in Iran that it probably does not wish to risk driving the Shah back wholly into the arms of the Americans by intervening in the Gulf sheikdoms or by backing Iraq too strongly against him. Finally, India remains more important for the Soviets than the Middle East, for only India can draw off the Chinese military presence on the Siberian border, and Soviet influence there has recently greatly increased. The Middle East remains important for the Soviets as a transit area to Asia and as an area to be denied to both the United States and China, but it may be relatively less important now that Soviet policy is primarily concerned with forging a *cordon sanitaire* of alliances around China *à la* John Foster Dulles.[35] Even so, assuming continued Arab radicalization and near total U.S. support of Israel, Moscow may continue to gain in the Middle East if only by profitting from probable U.S. losses.

China's policy in the Middle East, as elsewhere in the world, centered on containment of the Soviet threat. China thus wished to prevent the Soviet Union from operating via the Middle East against Chinese interests in East and Southeast Asia. Secondly, China wanted to lower the Western and particularly the American presence in the Middle East, provided only that it not be replaced by Soviet presence. Thirdly, China still, but to a lesser extent, continued to support the extremist fedayeen.

China's primarily anti-Soviet Middle Eastern policy was carried out both in the region and on its periphery. In the Middle East, China aided the fedayeen for fifteen years, but was never their exclusive supplier. It was never able to set up reliably pro-Maoist cadre parties within the fedayeen, and they have now become impotent and disorganized. Thus, although China constantly denounces the Soviets for allegedly conspiring with the Americans for a Middle Eastern settlement at Arab expense, more recently Peking welcomed approaches from such an anticommunist Arab leader as Numeiry and attempted with considerable success to establish diplomatic relations with all Arab states, radical or not. China had supported the only two guerrilla movements now operational in the Middle East. It was reportedly the main supporter of the PFLOAG (Popular Front for the Liberation of the Occupied Arab Gulf) in Dhofar against the Sultanate of Oman[36] and also aided the ELF (Eritrean Liberation Front) in Ethiopia. Moreover, the Chinese have not been as inhibited in the Persian Gulf as the Soviets out of concern for the Shah, but they still want good relations with him. The recent visit of Emperor Haile Selassie to Peking lowered Chinese support of the ELF, and the most recent reports from Dhofar indicated that the new Sultan, with significant British support, was making some progress against the PFLOAG insurgents, and that China was diminishing its support of them.[37] Even so, should leftist radicalism rise again in the Arab world, notably in the Gulf, it is still likely, provided that it serves Peking's anti-Soviet and anti-American objectives, that China will support it to a limited degree. In any case, Chinese attacks on Soviet "capitulationism" in the Middle East (as one may now expect with respect to Egypt) will continue to limit Soviet moves toward settlement there, while Arab weakness and Israeli intransigence make further Arab radicalization likely. Thus Chinese opportunities remain considerable.

Meanwhile, the Chinese have also attempted to contain the Soviets to the north and the south of the Middle East: in the Balkans and in Tanzania. Peking supports anti-Soviet states in the Balkans: Yugoslavia, Romania, and Albania. In Tanzania, where they have operated with sophistication and low profile, the Chinese are the most influential foreign power and are successfully constructing the Tanzam railway from Dar-es-Salaam to Lusaka.[38] How much effect this Chinese anti-Soviet pincers movement will have on the Middle East is uncertain; for the present, I think, not much. But strategically it has filled out their plan to contain the Soviets in the area.

In the near future, stagnation seems most likely in the Middle East. The Nixon visits to Peking and Moscow, plus Soviet inaction vis-à-vis his mining and bombing, and Sadat's expulsion of the Soviet advisors, have strengthened this tendency. In the longer run, however, it seems to me likely that as always before, Egyptian frustration, notably among the younger officers, will compel Sadat or his successor either to begin raids against the Israelis, with massive Israeli retaliation even with no Soviet support, or again to run the risk of a military coup. Cairo will delay this distasteful choice as long as possible. Eventually, however, it will probably choose raids. What will then happen is uncertain and fraught with danger. But assuming that either the Israelis again defeat the Egyptians or, more likely, that there is again, as in 1970, a Soviet-American imposed truce, the Arabs will once more relapse into humiliation and impotence. Leftist radical trends may then again rise within the Arab world, to the benefit of the Soviet Union and China.

Major Sino-Soviet rivalry in the Middle East is a development of the future. At present the Soviet Union is too strong and the Chinese far too weak. But even at current levels, Sino-Soviet rivalry there has had some significant results. It has limited Soviet-American and Arab-Israeli détente, for it has provided the Arabs an alternative, if minor, source of support, and, because of Moscow's interest in presenting itself as the center of world revolution, it has forced the Soviets to give more support to Arab revolutionaries there than they otherwise might.

As for the United States, its influence in the Arab world, although probably due to rise somewhat in Cairo and elsewhere after Sadat's conflict with Moscow, will in the long run probably continue to decline, because of radicalization and U.S. support of Israel. Moreover, the recent OPEC drive for acquisition by oil producing countries of shares in the western companies exploiting their oil fields, plus the potential instability of Saudi Arabia, Kuwait, and the Gulf Sheikhdoms, make the future of American oil companies in the Middle East, except for (much less profitable) technical aid, look bleak indeed. Worse, by the 1980s, the United States will become much more dependent on Middle Eastern oil. Washington will, however, be able to console itself for the time being by continued Arab division and impotence, Soviet-Arab friction, and, if the United States maintains naval and air superiority in the Mediterranean and the Persian Gulf, continued Soviet military inferiority in the area.

The Soviet-American confrontation in the Middle East will continue. But Soviet-American détente, now intensified by Sino-American rapprochement, will limit it and both super-powers will therefore probably continue effectively to restrain their allies. Moscow will continue to try to expand its influence, notably via Iraq, in the Gulf area, and to increase its naval presence in the Mediterranean. Thus while Soviet-American confrontation in the Middle East will still be limited by general Soviet-American détente, general Soviet-American détente will paradoxically still be limited by the Soviet-American confrontation in the Middle East.

South Asia

The 1971 Indian victory over Pakistan and the independence of Bangla Desh had two major results: India's predominance in the subcontinent, and greater Soviet influence in the area at the expense of Washington and Peking. In a larger historical perspective the Indian victory marked, first, a crushing, perhaps final defeat of the Muslims (who had conquered India from the west before the British arrived and who in 1947 had set up

Pakistan) by the Hindus (who had profited more than they from modernization and the 1947 partition). Second, it marked—at least for the near future—the end of substantial Western influence in India and the establishment of the Soviet Union as the most influential foreign power there. This is one of Brezhnev's major victories in foreign policy, for primary Russian influence over India has been a long-time Russian dream.[39]

Since India's independence, experts have differed about its prospects for political stability and economic growth. Optimists have stressed the remarkable continuity of Congress rule and a functioning parliamentary democracy. Pessimists have replied that ethnic hostility, the passivity of most Indians, and rapid population increase combined with slow economic growth are sooner or later bound to destabilize and eventually to fragment the Indian subcontinent. Indeed it seemed in 1970 that ethnic discord and leftist terrorism, notably in West Bengal were driving the Indian economy and polity into a downspin.

Mrs. Gandhi, who deserves the greatest credit for reversing this downward spiral, can best be understood as an elitist, ruthless, charismatic Kashmiri Brahmin. She used the Green Revolution to move Congress's mass base from the landowning and capitalist classes to the new kulaks, whom the Green Revolution created, notably in the Punjab, and to the rising small bourgeoisie who profit from them. (Yet the Green Revolution, like agricultural modernization in general, also has produced masses of surplus landless agricultural laborers—a new potential for radicalization.) In 1971, she brilliantly and ruthlessly eliminated her traditionalist "Syndicate" opponents in the old Congress machine. The pro-Soviet CPI was her satellite.

By 1970, West Bengal was in the greatest downward spiral of all, beset by large-scale pro-Peking Naxalite (CPML) terrorists, and with the essentially Bengali Nationalist Left Communists (CPM) in a majority and only kept from power by Mrs. Gandhi's imposition of "President's rule" (modified martial law). In 1970, however, Mrs. Gandhi decided to profit from the mass revulsion against Naxalite terrorism, to liquidate (i.e., kill or intern) them, reestablish law and order in West Bengal, and rejuvenate the decrepit West Bengal Congress—all of which she did. In 1971, she used the flush of Indian and Bengali nationalism over Bangla Desh to destroy the gerontocratic CPM in the 1972 West Bengal elections. Calcutta is much safer and cleaner than in 1971, and economic growth is slowly resuming under a remarkably young and dynamic Congress leadership.

Mrs. Gandhi's greatest triumph, the Indian defeat of Pakistan and a pro-Indian Bangla Desh, achieved through Indian arms and Soviet support, was primarily due not to her initiative, although certainly in large part to her skill, but rather to the blunders of the Pakistani leaders and the unviability of the Pakistan created by Jinnah and the British in 1947 and united only by Islam. A majority of Muslim Bengalis lived in poor, overpopulated East Pakistan, increasingly dominated by the minority of Muslim Punjabis, Pathans, Sindis, and Baluchis in West Pakistan (especially after the military takeover, for the officer corps was overwhelmingly West Pakistani). Moreover, the West, with its economy in the hands of a few families, exploited the East. The incompetence, corruption, and eventually the misplaced ruthlessness of the Western military toward the East did the rest. As early as 1950 the growth of East Bengali nationalism was held in check only by the military dictatorship of the West. The floods and cyclones of 1970 made the East Bengalis resent what they saw as too little West Pakistani aid. Finally, the initial bloody crushing by the West in 1971 of the onrushing Awami League movement toward autonomy in East Bengal, the arrest of its leader Sheikh Mujib, and the slaughter of so many of its supporters wrecked Pakistan. What else can the verdict on Yahya and his associates in Islamabad be but the old proverb: *Quem Deus vult perdere prius dementat?* Pakistan was unviable from the beginning, for an aggressive military minority can dominate a less aggressive nonmilitary majority only if they are contiguous and the minority is safe from defeat by a larger, other power. Pakistan is now hopelessly inferior to India, as much a Middle Eastern as a South Asian power. It speaks well for President Bhutto's realism, and for Mrs.

Gandhi's, that their July 1972 Simla summit meeting seems to have been at least a first, partial step toward Indo-Pakistani détente.

What of Bangla Desh? Is it the "international basket case" that one high Washington official allegedly termed it?[40] Although it is too early to tell, its prospects are not good. Poverty, hunger, floods, and typhoons, plus massive wartime destruction and the slaughter of much of its intelligentsia, have produced problems of enormous, perhaps insurmountable proportions. The Awami League is led by a group of Dacca lawyers, all better at rhetoric than administration, as is their leader, Sheikh Mujib. The left, although split and its pro-Chinese wing discredited by Peking's pro-Islamabad policy, is raising its head again. Indian influence there has already become unpopular, for the weak are never grateful to the strong, and the Muslim East Bengalis dislike the Hindu West Bengalis, who although fewer in number dominated them economically and culturally before the 1941 partition. No sufficient U.S. economic aid seems likely soon, nor will the Soviet Union probably take up all the slack. The prognosis for Bangla Desh remains unfavorable.[41]

So much for the setting in the subcontinent; what of the great powers—the United States, the Soviet Union, and China? Initially the American position in India was good, for Roosevelt had fixed Washington on an anticolonial course and most successor American administrations admired and aided India's "experiment in democracy." Moreover, as Sino-Indian hostility developed, Washington's adamant anti-Peking policy made it the more inclined to aid India, as Kennedy did in 1962. U.S.-Indian friendship foundered above all on Washington's military alliance with Pakistan, and its short-sighted policy of balancing hostile India and Pakistan on the subcontinent. As the 1960s went on, Washington's wooing of New Delhi gave way to indifference, if not scorn. Johnson and Nixon increasingly saw New Delhi as leftist, pro-Soviet, hostile to U.S. policy in Vietnam, and, more generally, as a part of that Third World in which the U.S. was becoming increasingly uninterested, and as a major and ineffective profiteer from the increasingly unpopular foreign aid program. India, conversely, became disenchanted with what it saw as anti-Indian, aggressive American policies.

Peking's initially good relations with India rapidly changed to hostility. Until China humiliatingly defeated India in 1962, New Delhi was Peking's major rival in Asia. Moreover, as China's power grew, it was unwilling to accept what it saw as Indian intrusions into territory that Britain had annexed from the Chinese Empire. Nehru's pre-1962 policy toward China was provocative out of weakness. Finally, to Peking, India was at first pro-American (i.e., in favor of China's then major enemy) and later pro-Soviet as well (i.e., in favor of China's other, now most dangerous foe). And, as the influence of the United States in New Delhi declined, that of the Soviet Union rose; so that Chinese hostility to India increased and it strengthened its ties with Islamabad, a development that further accentuated Sino-Indian tension. In the long run, Peking probably expects or at least believes the breakup of India into its component ethnic parts to be possible. Moreover, China probably feels that all Bengalis, East and West, are bound eventually to be hostile to the Hindi supremacy in New Delhi. Therefore, the Chinese probably argue, they can afford to be pro-Pakistani, for either one or both Bengals will eventually want their support.

The Soviets have been the great external profiteers from the recent history of the subcontinent. Modern Russia has always wanted to dominate the subcontinent, or at least to deny hegemony there first to Great Britain, then to the United States, and more recently to China. In the 1950s, India, like Egypt, was one of the first and most important targets of Khrushchev's drive for influence in the Third World. The main Soviet instrument of influence in India, as in Egypt, was arms and economic aid. Moscow also adroitly took advantage of the United States' alliance with Pakistan, its increasing uninterest in India, India's hostility to Pakistan and fear of China, and its own rising power. The Soviets also managed to mediate the 1965 Indo-Pakistani war and support India strongly in the 1971 war, thus largely destroying Western influence in India, and even ending up with reasonably good relations with Pakistan as well. All in all, this was a remarkable achievement, one of which Peter the Great would have been proud.

The United States, on the other hand, suffered a further sharp decline in its position in Delhi as a result of its "tilting toward Pakistan" during the Bangla Desh secession and the resultant Indo-Pakistani war. Washington's support of Pakistan worsened its relations with India more than if it had remained genuinely instead of only ostensibly neutral. But the basic reason why India recently moved further away from Washington and closer to Moscow was another one: Washington's rapprochement with Peking at a time when Peking remained hositle to New Delhi. India could therefore no longer depend on the United States for support against China. Washington's concern over rising Soviet power and its recognition of Chinese fear of the same made it give priority to rapprochement with Peking over its position in India. New Delhi therefore had no realistic alternative but to improve its relations with Moscow, whose hostility to Peking remained near total and on whom, therefore, India could best rely for help against China. Yet India is not and in all probability will not become a Soviet satellite, for it is now too self-confident and too distrustful of Soviet power and purpose.

Indeed, New Delhi continues to want to improve its relations with Peking. But Chinese hostility to India and its Soviet ally have so far prevented this. After Mao, however, a new Chinese leadership may feel that total hostility toward India, thus abandoning it to Moscow, is as counterproductive as total hostility toward Moscow itself. As to Washington, both India and the United States can also hardly have any interest in total hostility, which only makes India more dependent on Moscow than either New Delhi or Washington desires. (The United States remains, however, a convenient enemy around which Mrs. Gandhi can unify India, while India for the United States is peripheral—too far from the Middle East and the Pacific to be a vital area.) Indeed, Iran (toward whom Pakistan may well move) and Thailand are probably still more important for Washington. Even so, in its foreign policy—as lacking in influence as that is—India will henceforth be more inclined to support Soviet and to oppose American aims.

Thus, in the broadest sense the rise in Soviet influence in India was a direct, rapid, and probably inevitable result of the Sino-American rapprochement as well as of Mrs. Gandhi's successful campaign against Pakistan. What remains uncertain is India's future course and fate. At a meeting in Moscow in 1961 Khrushchev said sneeringly to Chou En-lai, "We have lost an Albania and you have gained an Albania." Whether or not Mao or Nixon will be able to say the same to Brezhnev, and with the same self-satisfied sneer, remains unclear.

Southeast Asia

Vietnam has long been influenced by, and played a significant role in, Sino-Soviet-American relations.[42] Until 1972, Moscow and Peking competed for the favor of Hanoi, and therefore aided it against Washington. Thus, the Vietnam War worsened Soviet-American, Sino-American, and also Sino-Soviet relations. But Nixon's successful détente with Peking and Moscow made both, even after he mined Haiphong, give preference to their successful relationship with the United States over aid to Hanoi. This contributed to the October 1972 Washington-Hanoi agreement in principle on a compromise peace. How and why did this agreement occur?

In 1965, the U.S. intervened in Vietnam primarily to stop what it saw as Chinese-sponsored expansionism. (In retrospect, even if this estimate were then correct, it was no longer so after the September 1965 coup in Djakarta; the decisive blow to whatever ambitions Peking had in Southeast Asia.) But the United States, perhaps inevitably, continued to fight ineffectively against the Viet Cong, and the war became America's Achilles heel. It resulted, as Richard Lowenthal has written, in "grave damage to its economic health, its social cohesion, its relative military strength and its capacity for diplomatic action."[43]

Until 1972, Washington's hope that Moscow, or Peking, or both, could and would effectively influence Hanoi toward a settlement proved groundless. Neither had any reason to help Washington to end the war on anything but terms very favorable to Hanoi. Hanoi itself always realized that the war would be won or lost in American public opinion. It did so well in this respect, and in the war itself, that until mid-1972 it continued to insist on unilateral and total U.S. abandonment of Saigon. Indeed, this was still the main calculation behind Hanoi's April 1972 offensive.

Hanoi had always tried to maintain maximum, "neutralist" independence from Moscow and Peking. By balancing between them, it tried to get maximum military and economic aid from each and to influence both against détente with Washington. Sino-Soviet worldwide competition, especially in support of national liberation movements, helped. Peking and Moscow wanted to expel U.S. influence from Southeast Asia but each was determined that it not be replaced by the other.

Until 1971, one key thread ran through Hanoi's relations with Moscow and Peking: its success in manipulating them against each other in order to enhance its own independence and power. But beginning with Kissinger's July 1971 visit to Peking and renewed signs of Soviet-U.S. détente, there developed a conflict of interest between Hanoi (for whom Washington remained the main enemy) and Moscow and Peking (for whom each was the main enemy of the other). Each consequently gave priority to détente with Washington over Hanoi. By 1972, therefore, Hanoi feared that both the Soviet Union and China would limit their aid to North Vietnam. The North Vietnamese therefore decided to launch their spring 1972 offensive before this occurred, and also to sabotage Nixon's summit détente diplomacy.

The initial April 1972 North Vietnamese successes over Saigon's forces reminded some observers of the 1949 Kuomintang debacle: South Vietnamese officers fled, troops panicked, and, had Giap been less cautious, he could probably have overrun Hué. But Hanoi miscalculated in five important respects: the massive, effective U.S. tactical air support in the South; the remarkably effective U.S. mining and bombing of the North (and the Soviet and Chinese inaction in its face); its own inability to effectively use Russian tanks and artillery; and, given overwhelming U.S. air support, the over-all fighting quality of the South Vietnamese army (ARVN). ARVN's record was spotty; without massive U.S. air support, Hanoi would probably have defeated them. Most of ARVN fought fairly well, however, while the North Vietnamese made many tactical errors in their use of tanks and artillery. By mid-1972 the conventional North Vietnamese assault had been contained and Quang Tri recaptured. But major damage had been done to pacification, notably in the Delta, and Vietnamization had been shown to be at best only a partial success. In short, Hanoi had not won most of its military objectives, but had won many of its political ones.

Yet Hanoi did not win its main objective: to defeat and demoralize ARVN and Saigon and thus to get U.S. public opinion to force the Americans to remove Thieu and withdraw. Nor did it successfully sabotage Nixon's détente with Peking and Moscow. Moreover, by mid-1972, North Vietnam was suffering seriously from the U.S. mining and bombing, and from the resultant lower level of Soviet and Chinese aid. In addition, we may assume that both Moscow and Peking by then were trying to persuade Hanoi to compromise. Finally, by September 1972, it was quite clear to the North Vietnamese that Nixon would decisively defeat McGovern in the autumn U.S. presidential elections, and thereafter be even less restrained by domestic opposition to the bombing and mining of North Vietnam. In Hanoi's view, perhaps the most important factor was its partial success in the April 1972 offensive, which had probably convinced the North Vietnamese leadership that, while military victory was not likely as long as U.S. air power backed Saigon, political victory within a reasonable period was likely once the United States withdrew. And, from the point of view of timing, Hanoi had every interest, once it had decided to compromise, to do so before the U.S. presidential elections on November 7, 1972, when a compromise would be electorally useful to Nixon.

Nixon's policy in Vietnam had always been to negotiate a compromise peace that would get the United States out and give the South Vietnamese anticommunists a credible chance of political survival. Their far from good performance in early 1972 had shown that their chances of survival with U.S. air power were not too encouraging, but that to guarantee their survival without it would take years. Moreover, the setbacks administered by Hanoi's April 1972 offensive to Vietnamization made Nixon's desire for a compromise and U.S. extrication even stronger. Thus, by late summer 1972 the Vietnamese context made a compromise peace seem more desirable to both Hanoi and Washington.

Nixon's summit visits to Peking and Moscow, combined with his bombing and mining of North Vietnam, and the Soviet and Chinese inaction in the face of it, had transformed the international context of the Vietnam War. First, and most significantly, these actions had downgraded the war's importance for Washington, Moscow, and Peking. They had made clear that the three major external powers would not allow the war to result in a confrontation among them or to interfere with Sino-American and Soviet-American détente; that they were implicitly agreed that the war should be ended as soon as possible by compromise; and that Moscow and Peking should exert pressure on Hanoi, and Washington on Saigon, toward this end. Thus Nixon had downgraded the war and made any "domino" effect that might result from Saigon's eventual collapse much less dangerous to U.S. interests.

At the same time both domestic and international factors in the Vietnamese situation were pushing Hanoi and Washington toward a compromise peace. Saigon, badly hurt by the North Vietnamese offensive and more clearly than ever dependent on U.S. air power, was in no position to resist the compromise indefinitely.

The terms of settlement, as set forth in October 1972, are a genuine compromise, a "cease fire in place", and very likely, a *de facto* partition of the South (with, however, Saigon initially controlling 90 percent of the population). Hanoi conceded the most. It abandoned its demand for a political settlement simultaneous with a cease fire (i.e., its demand for Thieu's removal and a tripartite coalition government in Saigon, including Viet Cong and neutralists as well as anticommunists). Rather, in contrast to Hanoi's previous demands, Thieu and his government will remain in power. There are provisions for international control. The Council for Reconciliation can act only by unanimous vote; i.e., Thieu can veto its actions. U.S. military supplies, for replacement purposes, can continue to come to Thieu, and there is no limit on his U.S. economic aid. (But neither are there limits on Soviet or Chinese military aid to Hanoi.) Nor is there any firm requirement for Saigon to liberate its political prisoners. Washington abandoned its demand that North Vietnamese troops leave South Vietnam; i.e., it agreed to *de facto* partition. (But there may be some understanding on mutual reduction of North and South Vietnamese forces in South Vietnam.)

The prospects for this compromise are most unclear. It is far from certain that most of its provisions, such as the proposed Council of National Reconciliation and effective international supervision, will become effective. It may even eventually collapse and guerrilla fighting resume.

For North and South Vietnam, in any case, the struggle will at least for a time become political instead of military, but it will continue. Whether South Vietnam can be modernized *à la* South Korea and resist takeover by Hanoi, or whether its fragmentation, corruption, and traditionalism are endemic and fatal, remains to be seen. For although the majority of South Vietnamese probably do not want to be under North Vietnamese or Viet Cong control, revolutions are won or lost by minorities, and up to now Hanoi and the Viet Cong have had social revolution and to a large extent nationalism on their side. The fates of Laos and Cambodia will depend on the outcome of the Vietnamese struggle. Their future is equally uncertain.

Thailand, initially concerned about the North Vietnamese offensive and the lack of consultation by Washington before the Peking and Moscow visits, was reassured by Nixon's drastic response to Vietnam. The insurgency in northern and eastern Thailand, largely Sino-Thai led and Peking-supported, has recently become more serious, and Bangkok shows no great signs of striking at its root causes. The major Thai concern remains its four million ethnic Chinese, and thus Bangkok is unlikely to prefer Peking to Washington. In the very long run, particularly if Washington disengages from the area, Thailand's hopes rest on neutrality of Southeast Asia under ASEAN.

On balance, Hanoi's long range prospects after peace seem to me to be better than Saigon's. More important though, while the final outcome in Vietnam like the succession to Mao Tse-tung remains one of the unknowns of international politics, its international significance has considerably declined.

Japan

Japan, not China, is in the near future the world's only potential third superpower.[44] It is also the most important area of the world where Chinese, Soviet, and American policies actively intersect. Finally, in no other country is the discrepancy between economic and technological power and military near impotence so glaring, or can the first be so rapidly, and for the world balance of power so decisively, turned into the second.

It is often said, particularly in Washington, that Japan is geographically too small and emotionally too pacifist to go nuclear, and that its trade ties with the United States and its fear of the Soviet Union and China preclude any *bouleversement des alliances*. Therefore, the argument concludes, "Japan has no other place to go." But the same argument was also put forward in the 1930s. Historically, although it normally moves slowly and by consensus, Japan has on occasion drastically changed its foreign policy. Japanese nationalism is rising. No successful alliance has ever faced such a communications gap as the Japanese-American one. Conversely, Japanese cultural ties with China are centuries old. It is thus risky to assume that Japan will necessarily behave in terms of how Washington or any Western observer sees Japanese national interests.

As of now, however, Japan's primary economic and defense concerns remain its trade and alliance with the United States. Japan is not soon likely to abandon either unless it concludes that U.S. policy compels it to do so. Yet rising Japanese nationalism demands a foreign policy less dependent on the United States. As Dean Acheson remarked of postwar Britain, Japan has lost an empire but not yet found a role. It is still searching for a national goal nobler than massive economic growth that will give it a new sense of identity, pride, and mission. This lack of a goal, when added to the alienation arising from the hectic rate of highly bureaucratized technological change and the resultant tension between the traditional and super modern aspects of Japanese society, make for increasing instability in Japanese society and polity.

Japan's search for a new goal was greatly intensified by the two "Nixon shocks" in the summer of 1971: the announcement, without any previous consultation with Tokyo, of his visit to Peking; and his taking the dollar off gold and imposing a temporary ten per cent surtax on imports, thus forcing a reevaluation of the yen. The results for the Japanese-American alliance have been almost wholly negative. Japanese-American relations will never again be the same. Even before these two "shocks" they were worsening somewhat because of rising economic competition. The fault was on both sides: the Japanese were far too slow in liberalizing American investment and in voluntarily limiting their exports to the United States, plus they greatly underestimated the American response to their massive and rising favorable balance of trade vis-à-vis the United States. The United States was too slow in correcting its inflation, its declining productivity, and its consequently less competitive position in international trade. The most dangerous trend in Japanese-American relations is the revival in the United States, especially in business and labor, of pre-1941 anti-Japanese feelings. With respect to the Sino-American détente, Tokyo hoped to continue to separate politics from economics in its relations with China. Washington, menaced by rising Soviet power and forced by domestic opinion to wind down its involvement in Southeast Asia, decided to improve its relations with China in order to compensate for these two developments. The cost was a worsening of American relations with Japan, through absence of consultation, and in large part, one may assume, because Japan would not help Washington compensate for the developments that were unfavorable to the United States.

Pressure in Japanese business and intellectual circles for improving relations with China had already been rising before 1971. Historically, Japan has felt culturally inferior, although technologically superior, to China. It was becoming more interested in trade with China in order to diversify its enormous but endangered foreign trade with the United States. Peking was convinced that Japan would not indefinitely remain a military dwarf. Memories of Japan's predatory conquest of China remained vivid in the Chinese Communist gerontocracy, and Mao and Chou have recently feared that declining U.S. pressure in Asia would be replaced by rising Japanese power; and thus their main ambition, to be the dominating power in East and Southeast Asia, would be frustrated. They feared this above all with respect to Taiwan, the recovery of which was one of their principal foreign policy objectives, and which, they calculated, might, after Chiang Kai-shek's death, fall into the hands of a Taiwan independence movement which would become a satellite of Japan. They feared the same in South Korea subsequent to an American withdrawal. Thus, China wanted to weaken the Japanese-American alliance, to prevent a Japanese-Soviet alliance, and to execute a rapprochement with Washington *inter alia* to worsen Japanese-American relations, and only thereafter to improve relations with Peking. Thereby, Peking hopes, it will get both Japanese technology and eventually establish Chinese hegemony in East and Southeast Asia.

Russo-Japanese relations have been hostile ever since both fought over the division of the declining Chinese Empire. Both are now technologically, and the Soviets militarily, the strongest powers in East Asia. The Soviet Union fears Japanese economic and technological power and its potential conversion into a military power. It sees Japan allied with and dependent upon its most powerful enemy, the United States, and perhaps in the future on its most dangerous foe, China. In 1945 the Soviets annexed the Kurile islands and Southern Sakhalin from Japan. Tokyo, pushed on by nationalistic pressures, demands some of the Kuriles back, a concession Moscow has so far not been prepared to make.

Recent developments, however, have opened the prospect of improvement in Soviet-Japanese relations. Moscow would like Japanese technology and credits to help close its technological gap, and specifically to help develop Siberia. Japan would like more trade and investment with the Soviet Union. But Japanese investment in Siberia has been slow, for the Soviets have been bureaucratically cautious and fearful of a Japanese presence too close to their Pacific Coast.[45] In 1972, the Soviets saw improvement of their relations with Japan as the most obvious and rapid countermove to the Sino-American rapprochement. Therefore Soviet Foreign Minister Gromyko visited Tokyo and agreed to negotiate a Soviet-Japanese peace treaty. The most recent reports indicate that Moscow may be prepared to return four of the Kuriles to Japan.[46] Tokyo fears that a Japanese rapprochement with Moscow would worsen Japan's relations with Washington and Peking. The Kurile issue still remains a serious obstacle to normalization of Soviet-Japanese relations. Mutual estrangement and mistrust are still great, and a rapid Soviet-Japanese rapprochement is therefore unlikely.

The two "Nixon shocks" were major blows to the Sato government and to the Japanese elite's self-esteem and trust in their U.S. reliance. Subsequent attempts on both sides to counteract them, including Henry Kissinger's recent visit to Japan, have been only partially successful. They intensified sentiment in Japan for improving relations with China and triggered several independent Japanese foreign policy moves: recognition of Bangla Desh and of Outer Mongolia before the United States, and the dispatch of a mission to Hanoi over U.S. objections.

The July 1972 election of Tanaka as Japanese Prime Minister may well represent a major watershed in postwar Japanese history and in particular in foreign policy. Tanaka is a self-made man, the first postwar prime minister to be neither a university graduate nor a bureaucrat; a relatively young, confident nationalist. Although his cabinet is still largely composed of elderly LDP notables, his policies are likely to move gradually but surely toward more emphasis on social and environmental problems at home and toward a more independent policy abroad. Although he still feels that Japan's primary alliance is with the United States, he will be a far less unconditional supporter of U.S. policies than Sato or his defeated rival Fukuda. Even so, the process of building a new foreign policy consensus will take some time.

Tanaka has responded to the rising tide of Japanese nationalism to some extent. He has therefore moved rapidly to reestablish relations with China. He reflects the current Japanese public and establishment priority for normalization of relations with Peking, rising out of historic cultural ties and Japanese guilt feelings over the Sino-Japanese War. Sino-Japanese normalization will have its problems, however. Moreover, Tanaka is determined not to lag behind the U.S. rapprochement with China and not to allow Peking to manipulate him against the United States. He has therefore decisively broken off relations with Taiwan. Finally, he is imitating Nixon by using improvement with Peking to get improvement with Moscow and vice versa. But the prospects for Soviet-Japanese détente remain unclear: they will primarily depend upon Moscow's concern over a Sino-Japanese détente.

Japan will remain a proponent of international détente and stability, if only because of her enormous dependence on foreign trade and above all on import of energy. She is and will remain the prime victim of OPEC, about which she can do little. Moreover, in the aftermath of Moscow's Haiphong humiliation, during the 1970s she, like the United States, will probably be faced by a rapidly increasing Soviet fleet in the Pacific and Indian Oceans, near her shores and astride her vital sea routes. What the United States will do about this will soon become an important factor in American-Japanese relations. The détente in the Korean peninsula (of which more below) will improve Japan's security situation, for a new Korean conflict has been one of her major worries. Should it and general international détente continue, Japan will probably want the United States to lower its naval and air presence in Japan. Japanese-U.S. economic relations will remain serious, and indeed Tokyo cannot anticipate that Nixon will allow the present multibillion dollar U.S. trade deficit with Japan to

52

continue much longer. Given Japan's potential domestic instability and the uncharted seas of foreign policy into which she is beginning to venture, one should not be overly confident about the future of Japanese-American relations. Japanese adjustment into a double triangular world in which Japan improves its relations with Moscow and Peking but still retains its primary security alliance with the United States, its primary economic competitor, will be difficult at best. If handled badly by the United States, Japan could well drift toward neutralism and nuclear rearmament.

Korea

Korea is the main area where the Soviet Union, China, the United States, and Japan intersect and compete. Until recently the impact of the great powers on the Korean peninsula intensified Pyongyang's and Seoul's mutual hostility. Most recent international developments have, however, contributed to its partial reduction. Indeed, they were the first (the Soviet-Egyptian crisis was the second) regional result of Sino-Soviet-American developments.[47]

Both Korean states are classic products of the Cold War. Kim Il-song's North Korea has been the most xenophobic, extremist, and militarist of all communist states. Until 1971, he seemed determined to bring down the Pak government in Seoul by guerrilla harassment. While South Korea remained adamantly hostile toward North Korea and entirely reliant upon the United States, Kim, like Ho Chi-minh fiercely nationalist and disillusioned by the lack of decisive Soviet and Chinese support in the Korean War, as was Ho by the 1954 Geneva peace settlement, skillfully maneuvered between Moscow and Peking and thereby gained independence from both. Like Ho, Kim was pro-Chinese in the late 1950s; more pro-Soviet after Khrushchev's fall, the U.S. escalation in Vietnam, and Mao's exclusivism during the Cultural Revolution; and again more pro-Chinese after 1969. He also shared Peking's concern over the rising power of Japan.

By late 1970, however, Korean and international factors

began to move Pyongyang and Seoul toward détente. Domestically, Kim's regime had acquired more stability and independence from Moscow and Peking, yet its campaign of guerrilla harassment against the South was clearly failing. Kim thus felt compelled to turn toward the other alternative, détente, in order to make progress toward his major single, if unrealistic, personal goal: the unification of Korea within his lifetime. In particular, he hoped that détente would push a wavering Washington into total troop withdrawal from the Korean peninsula. In the South, conversely, Pak wanted to enhance his security against North Korean harassment, the more so because, over his protests, Washington had in 1970 withdrawn 20,000 out of the 60,000 American troops in South Korea—thus, as in West Germany (whose parallels with and differences from South Korea, the only other divided nation where détente has set in, are most instructive)—raising for Seoul (as for Bonn) the menacing specter of total U.S. withdrawal while Pyongyang still remained hostile. Moreover, although fear of North Korean attack, going back to the overrunning of almost all South Korea in 1950, remains deep in South Korea; Seoul was more stable and in the midst of rapid economic growth, which would benefit from transfer of expenditures from the military to investment and rising debt service payments.

Internationally, in 1971 and 1972 both Kim and Pak realized that Sino-American and Soviet-American détente threatened them with isolation. Moreover, for North Korea it signalled the end of any hope of Soviet and/or Chinese support for armed struggle against the South and foreshadowed pressure on Pyongyang from both Moscow and Peking for a move toward détente with the South. For Seoul, conversely, détente increased the prospect of further major U.S. troop withdrawals and, should Pak maintain his cold war policies, of the decline, if not the end of U.S. aid for South Korean military modernization. This aid would be necessary for Seoul to gain military parity with Pyongyang. U.S. prospective withdrawal was dangerous for Seoul because it would deprive South Korea of its major single advantage over the North—the presence of U.S. tactical nuclear weapons in the peninsula and on U.S. ships offshore. Finally, both Pyongyang and Seoul, like Peking and Moscow (and to some extent Washington) were increasingly concerned over the rising economic and technological (and therefore potentially military) power of Japan, which had ruthlessly colonized Korea until 1945. Seoul was worried about Japanese economic penetration, and both Seoul and Pyongyang feared that U.S. withdrawal and increasing Soviet and Chinese disinterest, respectively, would leave a power vacuum which only Japan could and would fill. By 1972, in short, all of the major powers impinging on South and North Korea were for détente in the peninsula, and so were Kim and Pak.

A reasonably definitive analysis of the actual moves of Pyongyang and Seoul toward détente awaits further research. The Korean penchant for secrecy and conspiracy will make this most difficult. Although it is unclear whether Pyongyang or Seoul initiated the détente in the peninsula, it is clear that Pyongyang has throughout taken the more aggressive and Seoul the more cautious line. After gestures from both sides in late 1970 and early 1971, including a major North Korean reunification proposal at a time when East Germany had long since foresworn reunification for *Abgrenzung* (i.e., permanent separation), preliminary Pyongyang-Seoul Red Cross negotiations began in the latter year.

What was far more surprising, and indeed, by its speed, secrecy, and in my view brilliance, was the joint July 4, 1972, Pyongyang-Seoul communiqué, a result of secret visits to Pyongyang by, of all people, South Korea's CIA chief Lee Hu-rok, followed by the visit of a North Korean emissary to Seoul during spring 1972. The communiqué's highlighting of mutual commitment to peaceful Korean unification, although surely a very long range perspective indeed, did testify to the enormous strength of Korean nationalism. As it stated, in words unwelcome to East Berlin, to its imperial center in Moscow, or, for that matter, to any Marxist-Leninist true believer, ". . . As a homogenous people, a great national unity shall be sought above all, transcending differences in ideas, ideologies, and systems. . . ."[48] (It reflected, also, the fact that Korea, far more than Germany or even Vietnam, is a historically, culturally, linguistically, and regionally homogenous nation with a long, proud tradition, made stronger by its centuries-long struggle against Chinese, Mongol, Mancha, then Japanese, and finally, for North Korea, against Soviet and Chinese influence.)

What are the significance and prospects of this dramatic move? The primary objectives of both Pyongyang and Seoul are security, independence, and protection against Korea's three traditional major enemies: Russia, China, and Japan, plus, for Pyongyang, insurance against U.S. support of any action by Seoul against it. Seoul can best guard its independence by alliance with the strongest friendly distant power, the United States. Pyongyang, which has so far been neither able nor willing to do likewise, must balance between Russia and China and try to avoid too great hostility to Japan. Japan's vital security interests require that South Korea remain outside Russian or Chinese control. Washington finds its troop presence in South Korea useful to check Russia and China today and perhaps Japan tomorrow. Yet domestic U.S. pressures for troop withdrawals and rising South Korean military capability make its indefinite continuation doubtful, at least at anywhere near the present level. The present partial Pyongyang-Seoul détente, the single most important regional dividend to date of Sino-American and Soviet-American détente, has diminished the previous dangers of renewed hostilities in the Korean peninsula and thereby improved the position of all four major powers involved.

Other Regions

I will not discuss at any length in this essay the interaction of recent Sino-Soviet-American developments with events in Latin America and Africa, for in my view they have not been important.[49] First, both continents are too far away from the principal areas of major power confrontation. Latin America, with the exception of Cuba and to a small extent now of Chile, does not have major Soviet or Chinese influence. The weakness of African states and their intractability vis-à-vis foreign powers (except France) has made them less interesting to the three major powers.

As for Latin America, Fidel Castro's economic crisis and his unsuccessful sponsorship of guerrilla warfare in Latin America, his resultant rapprochement with the Soviet Union, and his recent cultural repression have lowered his appeal in Latin America as elsewhere. The Chinese have almost entirely concentrated on anti-Soviet operations, with little success. The Soviets, further encouraged by the coming to power of Allende in Chile, have supported the Latin American Communist parties' *via pacifica* policies and improved their relations with Latin American governments.

American policy in Africa, except for Ethiopia and Zaïre, is much less active than it once was. The Soviets and the Chinese continue to support and contend for influence within the various African liberation movements, but the rising power of South Africa has made them, and Soviet and Chinese policies toward them, more holding operations than ones with prospects of rapid success. Moreover, radical African states have increasingly given way to more technocratically inclined military dictatorships, less amenable to Soviet and Chinese influence. Nor is it likely that the Tanzam railway will give China decisive influence in either Zambia or Tanzania. The only foreign power with major influence in Africa is neither the Soviet Union, China, nor the United States, but France. Africa remains unlikely to play any important role in Sino-Soviet-American relations.

PART THREE:

Some Policy
Implications for
the United States

The unsuccessful and prolonged Vietnam War, problems of race, poverty, inflation and balances of payments and trade, and the alienation of much of its intelligentsia have seriously limited U.S. freedom of action in foreign policy. Scaling down of U.S. overseas commitments and a balance of power policy have thus become inevitable. These were also desirable for foreign policy reasons, for massive American power has often been engaged (and not only in Vietnam) in areas where vital U.S. interests were at most only peripherally involved. The threat to vital U.S. interests from its two principal enemies, due to Nixon's successful balance of power policy and pursuit of détente, somewhat diminished in 1972. Even so, rising Soviet military power and Soviet influence in the Middle East and India gave Washington continuing cause for concern.

Nixon's new balance of power policy could not be a classical nineteenth century one, for China, a regional rather than a global power, was weaker than the Soviet Union, and although Washington's adversary relationship with both became limited, it still remained one of conflict. For these reasons, and also because of geopolitics, trade, and tradition, U.S. relations with its economically strong but militarily weak allies, Western Europe and Japan, remain in my view more important, even though U.S. economic competition with them makes their maintenance more difficult.

The Nixon administration has dealt successfully with its adversaries but less so with its allies. Continuing international détente is probable and desirable for America, for it furthers American security and economic interests. Washington has wisely pursued it by developing better relations with Moscow and Peking than either has with the other. While (correctly) denying any intent to do so, it has thus manipulated both to its advantage.

The greatest and indeed the only serious current U.S. foreign policy failure has been in its relations with Japan. Washington's economic shock to Tokyo was probably inevitable and the blame was on both sides. But the lack of consultation with Tokyo before the visit to Peking was unnecessarily damaging to U.S. interests. To say, as one often hears in Washington, that nonconsultation was necessary in order to bring the Peking visit off is incorrect, in my view, for three reasons. First, the Chinese if anything needed the visit more than Nixon did, and it was thus unlikely that they would have called it off merely because Nixon had consulted Sato previously about it. Nor could consultation with Japan not have been done secretly: there are many gradations between discussing it at length with the Japanese cabinet and telling Sato that it was forthcoming only a few minutes before it was publicly announced. Finally, the Chinese wanted to weaken the Japanese-American alliance through the visit, and, in large part because of Washington's lack of consultation, they succeeded. Behind all this, I fear, is a disturbing revival in American public opinion and even in some high quarters in Washington of the traditional American fascination with China and dislike of Japan. Let us hope that the verdict on all this will not be that old, sad one, "those who do not learn from history are condemned to repeat it." Restoration of cordial U.S. relations with Japan should be the first priority for U.S. foreign policy. It need not seriously interfere with successful U.S. détente with Moscow and Peking. Fortunately, there are some encouraging signs in this direction.

As to Korea, Nixon's balance of power policy has so far

been wholly successful. It will continue to be so insofar as he, or his successor, can successfully resist domestic U.S. pressure for rapid and unilateral, as opposed to gradual and balanced, U.S. troop withdrawal from South Korea.

The Nixon administration has significantly improved U.S. political relations with Western Europe, by full consultation and by largely giving up the Kennedy-Johnson priority for relations with the Soviet Union over relations with the West European states. Moreover, President Nixon has courageously and so far successfully resisted the neo-isolationist pressure of Senator Mansfield and others for massive U.S. unilateral troop withdrawals from Europe.

In two other major respects U.S. policy toward Europe has been less successful: trade and East-West relations. As to the former, the blame, as with Japan, is on both sides. Western Europe is in some respects in better economic health than the United States. EEC trade discrimination has hurt American industry and agriculture. Yet America defends Western Europe, strategically and conventionally, largely at its own expense. But American economic protectionism is not the answer to this problem: it will only lead to a trade war and hurt the U.S. economically. The forthcoming U.S.-EEC trade negotiations will be crucial in this respect.

As to East-West relations, the administration's initial, hardly concealed, and, in my view, basically unjustified distrust of Brandt's *Ostpolitik* has fortunately given way after the Berlin Agreement to support for it. Moreover, at the Moscow summit, Washington finally and sensibly agreed to a Conference on Security and Cooperation in Europe (CSCE) in return for Soviet agreement to MBFR negotiations. Washington should now adopt an energetic forward strategy for CSCE. Specifically, it should push forward vigorously toward an agreed NATO proposal for its agenda, including the establishment of a permanent European Security Commission and liberalization of communication between East and West. The U.S. has too long been negligent in allowing Moscow to run with this particular détente ball: it is high time that America does some running with it itself.

The urgency for new initiatives by the United States in the Middle East is less than it was a year ago, for the situation there has become less dangerous. Indeed, Sadat's July 1972 expulsion of the Soviet advisors potentially improved American leverage in Cairo. What is more, exactly Nixon's combination of initial flexibility toward Cairo, then total support of Israel, and finally facing down of and negotiating with Moscow, pushed Sadat to expel them. Logically, therefore, Washington should now help Sadat to take a more independent position toward the Soviet Union, Western Europe, and the United States.

But this is probably only a short-term perspective. In the long run, Sadat, or his successor, can hardly make peace with Israel before he has chanced at least one more round of hostilities. Even then, and assuming continued total U.S. support of Israel (i.e. as long as the U.S., alone among the Western powers is seen by even moderate Arabs to be wholly on the side of Israel) the Americans will in the long run lose, and the Soviets, albeit to a lesser extent, gain influence in the Arab world. The United States should, in its own interest, guarantee Israel's security but not its conquests. The longer the United States is seen by the Arabs to guarantee the latter, by lack of decisive action, the more Washington will hurt its own interests. After the U.S. presidential elections, one foreign policy priority for the new administration should be (but very likely will not be) to resume efforts to get the Israelis out of almost all of their conquered territories.

The Indian subcontinent is neither an area vital to U.S. security, nor one where the United States can expect to have major influence, now that India is predominant there and China remains hostile to India. Yet the Nixon administration unnecessarily, clumsily, and counterproductively "tilted" toward Pakistan—a losing horse. For the Nixon administration, as for many Americans, Pakistanis are more attractive than Indians. But, as with Japan, statesmen should rise above their sentiments. The United States should have been neutral in the Indo-Pakistani war, and needed to be nothing more in order not to interfere with U.S. détente with China. The best that can be done now is gradually to resume some economic aid to India, to give major relief aid to Bangla Desh, and to wait for the dust to settle.

Finally, Vietnam. Domestic opinion and U.S. world strategy require that Washington extricate itself from that unhappy country. On any scale of cost-effectiveness it has cost the United States in blood, treasure, and domestic comity far more than it is worth to U.S. interests. But the manner of extrication is important: it must be done in such a way that the Soviets and the Chinese do not get the impression that the United States is capitulating. For if they do, the risk of much more dangerous confrontations, notably in the Middle East, becomes too great. President Nixon was right to mine the harbors of North Vietnam, for a major American retaliation for Hanoi's massive invasion of South Vietnam was necessary. He has also been proven right, and his critics wrong, in his view that the mining would not unacceptably worsen U.S. relations with Moscow and Peking. (It did not, in large part, because of his détente with both.) On the contrary, the worldwide blow to Soviet and Chinese prestige as a result of their inaction thereafter would make any eventual victory by Hanoi in Indochina less damaging to U.S. worldwide interests. The pending compromise settlement now agreed to in principle by Washington and Hanoi is in my view desirable from the viewpoint of U.S. interests.

One of the lessons of the Vietnam War is that the United States should be less concerned about international stability *per se* and more about the protection of its own vital interests. The United States cannot save the world for democracy, and even if it could there is no reason why it should respond to such a self-proclaimed call to do so. American relations with Spain and Greece, Yugoslavia and North Korea, should be carried on, as those with all other countries in the world, democratic or not, in accord with U.S. national interests.

Alexis de Tocqueville wisely remarked that nothing is more difficult for a democracy than to carry on a consistent, rational foreign policy. The current American moralism, isolationism, and *trahison des clercs* make it doubly difficult. Yet the U.S. public will not support a purely Machiavellian *Realpolitik.* It must also have some higher, more idealistic, indeed ideological goal, or otherwise goals based on national interest will lose public support. But these goals, after Vietnam, clearly cannot be the pursuit of universal stability and democracy. There are, however, three other U.S. goals that together can provide a standard to which decent men can repair. The first is to reform U.S. society—its poverty, racial prejudice, drug addiction, and intellectual fanaticism—so that once more the United States will become a model to admire, not an example to fear. The second is to use more of America's wealth to aid the ill and hungry abroad. The third is to continue to intensify international détente. If the U.S. pursues all these successfully, while maintaining a reasonable deterrent posture against its enemies, Americans need not fear for the Republic.

64

NOTES

1. I have profited greatly from travels in Europe, the Middle East, and Asia in June and July 1972, for which I am grateful to *The Reader's Digest* and to its president, Hobart Lewis, and also to the Bureau of Cultural Affairs of the U.S. Department of State, which invited me to give lectures in Japan and Korea. I am also grateful for comments and discussions to John Batatu, Zbigniew Brzezinski, Satin Chakravarty, Francois Fejto, Marcus Franda, Ivan Hall, Pierre Hassner, Ilpong J. Kim, Han Kiuk, Chul Koh, Hidejiro Kotani, Fred Luchsinger, Viktor Meier, Lucian Pye, Hahm Pyong-choon, Edwin Reischauer, Samuren Roy, Kiichi Saeki, Dan Avni-Segre, Bhabani Sen Gupta, Slobodan Stankovic, Michel Tatu, Wolfgang Wagner, Richard L. Walker Kim Young-sun, and many others who must remain anonymous. None of them, however, is responsible for the contents of this essay: that responsibility is mine alone.
2. Cf. Doak Barnett, "The Changing Pattern of U.S.-China Relations," *Current Scene,* Apr. 10, 1972; Richard Lowenthal, "A World Adrift," *Encounter,* Feb. 1972; the articles on Sino-American relations in *Problems of Communism,* Nov.-Dec. 1971 and Jan.-Feb. 1972; Harry G. Gelber, "Peking, Washington, and the Pacific Balance of Power," *Pacific Affairs,* Oct. 1971; Harry Harding, Jr., "China: The Fragmentation of Power," *Asian Survey,* Jan. 1972; Michel Oksenberg, "How long a march together?," *Far Eastern Economic Review,* July 1, 1972; and William E. Griffith, *The Great Globe Transformed,* Part I, (Cambridge, Mass.; MIT Center for International Studies Monograph C/71-15, Oct. 1971) (with full bibliography). I have also benefited from papers by A. M. Halpern and Shinkichi Eto presented at the Fifth Conference of the Korean Institute for International Affairs, Seoul, July 11-13, 1972.
3. The most authoritative official statements of U.S. foreign policy in this and other respects are *United States Foreign Policy for the 1970s: The Emerging Structure of Peace,* a report by President Richard Nixon to the Congress, Feb.

1972, his interview in *The Reader's Digest* (Feb. 1972), and his long article, "The Real Road to Peace," *U.S. News and World Report*, June 26, 1972.

4. See especially Michel Tatu, *Le triangle Washington-Moscou-Pékin et les deux Europe(s)* (Paris: Casterman, 1972), and his previous 1970 Atlantic Institute paper, *The Great Power Triangle: Washington-Moscow-Peking*. For a recent authoritative Soviet viewpoint, see G. A. Arbatov, "Outlook for Soviet-American Detente," *SShA*, no. 2, Feb. 1972 (*JPRS* 55416, March 13, 1972.) See also Winfried Bottcher et al., eds., *Das grosse Dreieck, Washington-Moskau-Peking* (Stuttgart: Deutsche Verlags-Anstalt, 1971), and the brilliant review of research on conflict limitation and arms control by Pierre Hassner, "On ne badine pas avec la force," *Revue francais de science politique*, Dec. 1971.

5. Alain Jacob from Moscow in *Le Monde*, June 3, 1972.

6. That he (understandably) denied doing so should not be allowed to lessen one's estimate of his accomplishment.

7. Thomas W. Wolfe, "Soviet Interests in SALT," RAND P-4702, Sept. 1971.

8. The case that it will, and intentionally, was well put by Herbert Scoville Jr., in *The New Republic*, March 25, 1972.

9. Andrew J. Pierre, "America Down, Russia Up: The Changing Political Role of Military Power," *Foreign Policy*, Fall 1971.

10. Documentation: *The New York Times*, May 27, 30, June 3, 14, 1972; analysis: Michel Tatu in *Le Monde*, May 31, 1972.

11. The most authoritative analysis of recent Sino-Soviet developments is the excellent study by Harold Hinton, *The Bear at the Gate* (Washington, D.C.; American Enterprise Institute and Stanford, Calif.: The Hoover Institution, 1971), with full bibliography.

12. See my *The Great Globe Transformed, Part I* (MIT Center for International Studies Monograph, C/71-15, Oct. 1971) and "Kiev Attacks Ukrainian 'Pro-Chinese' Group," *Radio Free Europe Research*, March 10, 1972.

66

13. See the penetrating and comprehensive analysis by Heinz Timmermann, " 'Neue Einheit' im Weltkommunismus," *Berichte des Bundesinstituts fur ostwissenschaftliche und internationale Studien* (Cologne), 2/1972.

14. E.g., Ivanov in *Kommunist,* no. 17, Nov. 1971, (JPRS 54945, Jan. 14, 1972); Sobolov in *Mezhdunarodnaya zhizn',* no. 3, Feb. 22, 1971; and the convenient collection of Soviet reactions to the Nixon visit to Peking in *The Current Digest of the Soviet Press,* Mar. 22, 1972; cf. Jacob from Moscow in *Le Monde,* Dec. 17, 1971.

15. William E. Griffith, *The Great Globe Transformed, Part V, Europe* (Cambridge Mass.: M.I.T. Center for International Studies Monograph C/71-19, Oct. 1971) (with full bibliography); Francois Duchene, "The Future of Europe: Ways Forward," *The World Today,* Nov. 1971. See also the illuminating articles by Karl Birnbaum, Pierre Hassner, and Wolfgang Wagner in *International Journal* (Toronto), Winter 1971-1972. I have benefited in July 1972 from conversations in Paris, Geneva, Zurich, and Bonn, and from participation in the European-American Conference at Akademie Eichholz, Wesseling, June 5-7, 1972, sponsored by the Forschungsinstitut der Deutschen Gesellschaft für Auswärtige Politik.

16. Horst Mendershausen, *Western European Power: Mirage and Realities* (Southern California Arms Control and Foreign Policy Seminar, mimeo., April 1972).

17. See the excellent analyses by Richard Lowenthal, "The World Adrift," *Encounter,* Feb. 1972; and Harold B. Malmgren, "The New Posture in U.S. Trade Policy," *The World Today,* Dec. 1971.

18. Lawrence L. Whetten, *Germany's Ostpolitik* (London: Oxford, 1971); Wolfgang Wagner, "Aussichten der Ostpolitik nach dem Abschluss der Berlin-Verhandlungen," *Europa Archiv,* Feb. 10, 1972; Gerhard Wettig, "Zur sowjetischen Politik der europäischen Sicherheit vom Herbst 1970 bis Ende 1971," (Cologne: Bundesinstitut fur ostwissenschaftliche und international Studien, mimeo., Dec. 1971); Dieter Mahncke, "The Berlin Agreement: Balance and Prospects,"

The World Today, Dec. 1971; Michael Palmer, *The Prospects for a European Security Conference* (London: Chatham House, European Series no. 18, 1971), and "A European Security Conference: Preparation and Procedure," *The World Today,* Jan. 1972; Paul Frank, "Zielsetzungen der Bundesrepublik Deutschland in Rahmen europäischer Sicherheitsverhandlungen," and Uwe Nerlich, "MBFR in der europäischen Sicherheitspolitik," *Europa-Archiv,* March 10, 1972; Charles Andras, "The Seven Pillars of Europe (The Warsaw Pact and European Security in 1972)", *Radio Free Europe Research,* March 16, 1972; Christoph Bertram, *Mutual Force Reductions in Europe: The Political Aspects* (London: International Institute for Strategic Studies, Adelphi Paper no. 84, Jan. 1972).

19. Robert R. King, "A Lull in Romania's Relations with China?" *Radio Free Europe Research,* Feb. 15, 1972.
20. See especially K. F. Cviic, "The Outlook for Yugoslavia," *The World Today,* Dec. 1971, and an article by Slobodan Stankovic, "Die kroatische Krise-Triebkräfte und Perspektiven," *Osteuropa,* June 1972.
21. Paul Wohl, "Coolness Parts Albania, China," *The Christian Science Monitor.* May 5, 1972; F. Stephen Larrabee, "Changing Perspectives on the Balkans," *Radio Free Europe Research,* Dec. 9, 1971, and "Neue Entwicklungstendenzen auf dem Balkan," *Europa-Archiv,* March 10, 1972.
22. See the revealing unpublished report by Vasil Bilak to the KSC CC. Oct. 21, 1971, summarized in *Le Monde,* Feb. 12, 1972. Hungarian-Soviet differences have been exaggerated in the West; they have been only economic in nature. See Hanni Konitzer from Budapest in *Frankfurter Allgemeine Zeitung,* June 7, 1972.
23. See the Brezhnev speech to the Soviet Trade Union Congress, *Pravda,* Mar. 21, 1972.
24. See j.c.k. (Joseph C. Kun), "Peking's View of Western Europe," *Radio Free Europe Research,* Apr. 5, 1972.
25. See in general and for bibliographical citations my paper, *The Great Globe Transformed, Part IV, The Middle East* (Cambridge, Mass.: MIT Center for International Studies,

c/71-18, Oct. 1971). See also John C. Campbell and Helen Caruso, *The West and the Middle East* (New York: Council on Foreign Relations, Council Papers on International Affairs, 1972). I have also benefited from discussions in Tel Aviv, Jerusalem, Beirut, and Cairo in June 1972, and from the regular Middle Easten coverage by A.H. (Arnold Hottinger) in the *Neue Zurcher Zeitung* and by Eric Rouleau in *Le Monde*. My analysis of the most recent Middle Eastern developments, and especially of Sadat's July 1972 expulsion of the Soviet advisors from Egypt, was necessarily based on preliminary and incomplete reports, particularly because I was at that time travelling in Mexico and Central America. I relied primarily on *The New York Times,* especially on an analysis by Ihsan A. Hijazi from Beirut in the July 2 issue, and also on an excellent analysis by Jean-Francois Chauvel from Cairo in *Le Figaro,* July 19, 1972.

26. D.C. Watt, "The Persian Gulf—Cradle of Conflict?," *Problems of Communism,* May-June 1972.

27. *Radio Liberty Research,* Feb. 7. 1972; Eric Rouleau from Khartoum in *Le Monde,* weekly English ed., Mar. 4, 1972; Chou En-lai to the Sudanese delegation on Dec. 17, 1971, ("the Sudanese government and people have again smashed a foreign subversive plot") in *Peking Review,* Dec. 24 1971; and pro-Soviet attacks on Numeiry in the (pro-Soviet) *African Communist,* Fourth Quarter 1971.

28. See the perceptive reports from Cairo by Arnaud de Borchgrave in *Newsweek* Feb. 28, 1972; and especially A. H. [Arnold Hottinger] in *Neue Zurcher Zeitung,* Sept. 26, 1971, and May 30, 1972. Cf. Shlomo Slonim, "Egypt's Conflict of Alliances," *The World Today,* March, 1972.

29. Shimon Shamir, "The Marxists in Egypt," prepared for the Conference on the Soviet Union and the Middle East, Dec. 26-30, 1971, Shiloah Center for Middle East and African Studies, Tel Aviv University.

30. This was made clear by the April 4, 1972, memorandum of several moderate excolleagues of Sadat and by subsequent *Al Ahram* editorials by Heikal. See Hijazi from Beirut in

The New York Times, July 19, 1972.

31. The pro-Cairo *Al Moharrer* (Beirut) reported in July 1972 that Paris-Cairo weapons negotiations had been going on for a year, *The New York Times,* July 20, 1972.

32. For recent general surveys, see George Lenczowski, *Soviet Advances in the Middle East* (Washington, D.C.: American Enterprise Institute, 1971) and Walter Laqueur, "Russians vs. Arabs: The Age of Disenchantment," *Commentary,* April, 1972. For renewed Soviet cautioning of the Arabs against military action, see an apparently authentic report of a discussion between Soviet and Syrian CP officials in Moscow, as summarized from *Al Rayah* (Beirut) in *The New York Times,* June 30, 1972. For more bibliography, see my paper, *The Great Globe Transformed, Part IV, The Middle East* (Cambridge, Mass.: MIT Center for International Studies Monograph, C/71-18, Oct. 1971).

33. Morroe Berger, "The Arabs' Attitude to the West," *The Yale Review,* Winter 1972.

34. Paul Balta in *Le Monde,* Apr. 10, 1972, and *Le monde diplomatique,* April 1972.

35. Edward Luttwak, "Russia and China: A Logistic View of Soviet Policy," *The New Middle East,* March/April, 1972.

36. See R. M. Burrell, "Rebellion in Dhofar: The Spectre of Vietnam," *The New Middle East,* March/April, 1972.

37. Eric Rouleau from Aden in *Le Monde,* May 31, 1972.

38. George T. Yu, "Working on the Railroad: China and the Tanzania-Zambia Railway," *Asian Survey,* Nov. 1971.

39. David H. Bayley, "India: War and Political Assertion," and Robert Laporte Jr., "Pakistan in 1971: The Disintegration of a Nation," *Asian Survey,* Feb. 1972; W. Klatt, "The Indian Subcontinent After the War," *The World Today,* March 1972; Norman D. Palmer, "The New Order in South Asia," *Orbis,* Winter 1972; P.H. [Peter Hess] "Gestärktes Selbstvertrauen Indiens nach dem Krieg," *Neue Zürcher Zeitung,* Feb. 6, 1972; the symposium on the 1971 Indian elections in *Asian Survey,* Dec. 1971; M. Rashiduzzaman, "Leadership, Organization, Strategies and Tactics of the Bangla Desh Movement," *Asian Survey,* March 1972; Pran

70

Chopra, "Political Re-alignment in India," *Pacific Affairs,*
Winter 1971-1972; William Barnds, *India, Pakistan and the
Great Powers* (New York: Praeger, 1972) and "Moscow and
South Asia," *Problems of Communism,* May-June 1972;
William E. Griffith, *The Great Globe Transformed, Part II*
(Cambridge, Mass.: Center for International Studies MIT,
C/71-17, Oct. 1971) (with full bibliography); Marcus
Franda, *Radicalism in West Bengal* (Cambridge, Mass.: MIT
1971); Paul Brass and Marcus Franda, eds., *Radicalism in
South Asia* (Cambridge, Mass. MIT, 1973, forthcoming);
Bhabani Sen Gupta, *Communism in Indian Politics* (New
York: Columbia, 1972) and "Indian Communism," *Prob-
lems of Communism,* Jan.-Feb. 1972. For the Soviet
presence in the Indian Ocean, see Geoffrey Jukes, *The
Indian Ocean in Soviet Naval Policy* (London: IISS, Adelphi
Paper no. 87, May 1972). I have profited from comments
on an earlier draft by my colleague John Field and from
many talks with Paul Brass, Marcus Franda, Bhabani Sen
Gupta, and Myron Weiner and from discussions in New
Delhi, Katmandu, and Calcutta in June 1972.
40. U. Alexis Johnson at a WSAG meeting on Dec. 6, 1971, in
the "Anderson Papers," as published in *The Washington
Post,* Jan. 5, 1972.
41. Gerard Viratelle, "Le Bangla-Desh est-il mal parti?," *Le
Monde,* July 20, 1972 *et seq.*
42. Douglas Pike, "North Vietnam in 1971," *Asian Survey,* Jan,
1972; Allan E. Goodman, "South Vietnam and the New
Security," ibid., Feb. 1972; and especially Michel Tatu from
Saigon in *Le Monde* July 13 and 14, 1972 and "Qui a cédé?,"
ibid, Oct. 28, 1972. The most recent developments can be
followed in the press, especially *The Christian Science
Monitor.* I have benefited especially from conversations in
Saigon in June 1972 with their correspondent Donald
Southerland and AFP correspondent Felix Bolio, as well as
with many other Americans and Vietnamese, and also from
conversations in Hong Kong and Seoul with Robert Shaplen.
43. "A World Adrift," *Encounter,* Feb. 1972.

44. Joachim Glaubitz, "Japan im Schatten der amerikanisch-chinesischen Kontakte," *Europa-Archiv*, Feb. 10, 1972; Edwin O. Reischauer, "Fateful Triangle—The U.S., China, and Japan," *The New York Times Magazine*, Sept. 19, 1971; Lee W. Farnsworth, "Japan: The Year of the Shock," *Asian Survey*, Jan. 1972; Michel Tatu from Tokyo, "Le Japon cherche sa voie," *Le Monde*, June 10, 1972; Fritz Steck, "Japan—nicht mehr im stillen Winkel," *Neue Zürcher Zeitung*, May 28, 1972; Zbigniew Brzezinski, *The Fragile Blossom* (New York: Harper and Row, 1971). I also profited greatly from a conference sponsored by SAIS at Airlie House, Feb. 11-12, 1972, and particularly from the remarks there by Paul Langer of RAND, and from many discussions during a two week stay in Japan in June-July 1972. See also my *The Great Globe Transformed, Part II* (Cambridge, Mass.: Center for International Studies Monograph C/71-16, Oct. 1971) (with full bibliography).
45. See the authoritative analysis by Kiichi Saeki, President of the Nomura Institute of Technology and Economics (Kamakura), "Toward Japanese Cooperation in Siberian Development," *Problems of Communism*, May-June 1972.
46. Guillain from Tokyo in *Le Monde*, April 9, 10, 1972.
47. Robert Simmons, "North Korea: Year of the Thaw," and Chae-Jin Lee, "South Korea: Political Competition and Government Adaptation," *Asian Survey*, Jan. 1972. I have benefited from conversations in Seoul in July 1972, from participation there in the Fifth International Conference of the Korean Institute of International Studies, July 11-13, 1972, particularly from the papers by Prof. Kyung Won Kim of Korea University and Prof. Byung Chul Koh of the University of Illinois at Chicago Circle, and from discussions at the Asiatic Research Center of Korea University.
48. *The New York Times*, July 5, 1972.
49. See my *Latin America 1972* (MIT Center for International Studies Monograph, C/72-17, Oct. 1972).